Common Core Progress

English Language Arts

3

 **Sadlier School**

For additional online resources, go to sadlierconnect.com.

William H. Sadlier, Inc.
9 Pine Street
New York, NY 10005-4700

Printed in the United States of America.
ISBN: 978-1-4217-3053-0
4 5 6 7 8 9 10 WEBC 20 19 18 17 16

CONTENTS

continued next page

RL.3.4, RL.3.5, RL.3.6, RL.9,
RL.3.10, SL.3.1.a, SL.3.1.c,
SL.3.1.d, SL.3.4

L.3.5.a

RL.3.4, RL.3.5, RL.3.6, L.3.5.a

Unit 6   Text Types and Purposes:
Write Nonfictional Narratives

W.3.3.a–d, W.3.4, W.3.5, W.3.10

L.3.1.a, L.3.1.d–f, L.3.2.e

SL.3.1.a–d, SL.3.3

W.3.3.a–d, W.3.4, W.3.5, W.3.10,
L.3.1.a, L.3.1.d–f, L.3.2.e

Unit 7   Reading Informational Text:
Craft and Structure

RI.3.4, RI.3.5, RI.3.6, RI.9,
RI.3.10, SL.3.1.a, SL.3.1.c,
SL.3.1.d, SL.3.4

L.3.4.b

RI.3.4, RI.3.5, RI.3.6, L.3.4.b

W.3.1.a–d, W.3.4, W.3.5, W.3.10

L.3.1.a, L.3.1.g, L.3.1.i, L.3.2.f, L.3.2.g, L.3.4.d, L.3.6

SL.3.1.a–d, SL.3.3

W.3.1.a–d, W.3.4, W.3.5, W.3.10, L.3.1.a, L.3.1.g, L.3.1.i, L.3.2.f, L.3.2.g, L.3.4.d, L.3.6

RL.3.7, RL.3.9, RL.3.10, SL.3.1.a, SL.3.1.c, SL.3.1.d, SL.3.4

L.3.4.c

RL.3.7, RL.3.9, L.3.4.c

W.3.4, W.3.5, W.3.7, W.3.8, W.3.10

continued next page

Unit 11 Reading Informational Text:
Integration of Knowledge and Ideas

COMMON CORE STATE STANDARDS
CCSS

L.3.1.h–i, L.3.2.a

SL.3.1.a–d, SL.3.3

W.3.4, W.3.5, W.3.7, W.3.8, W.3.10, L.3.1.h–i, L.3.2.a

RI.3.7, RI.3.8, RI.3.9, RI.3.10, SL.3.1.a, SL.3.1.c, SL.3.1.d, SL.3.4

L.3.5.c

RI.3.7, RI.3.8, RI.3.9, L.3.5.c

RF.3.3.a–d, RF.3.4.a–c

W.3.2, W.3.4, W.3.5, W.3.6, W.3.7, W.3.8, W.3.10, SL.3.4, SL.3.6, L.3.1.f, L.3.1.i, L.3.2.a, L.3.2.g, L.3.3.a, L.3.3.b, L.3.6

Welcome

You have an exciting year ahead of you. You will be reading all kinds of different passages—in all sorts of formats—about interesting topics, such as heroes, natural disasters, and the solar system. You'll learn how to read more carefully so you can better understand what you read.

Writing is important, too. Suppose you want to give your opinion about an editorial you read, or compare two accounts of the same historical event. If you write well, you can communicate these ideas clearly. You will also see other students' writing and try to improve on it or use it as a model for your own work.

This book, *Common Core Progress*, will help you improve in both reading and writing, and maybe even do better in school. That's why it's called *progress*.

Have a great year!

Introducing UNIT 1

Since the earliest times, people have been telling each other stories. Many of the stories that have been passed down to us are fables, folktales, and myths. In this unit, you will read some of these stories about heroes from the past.

We don't know who first told these stories. Yet we still enjoy them. Each one has an important message for us. It might be a lesson on how to act toward other people, an inspiring tale that makes us stand up for what is right, or a way for people of former times to explain things in nature that they could not understand. As you read each story, you will pick out details that tell where and when things happen. You will learn who the characters are and what they are like. You will learn to ask and answer questions about the story's conflict and how it is solved.

Connecting details in stories will help you better understand the stories of long ago. Then you can pass them along to someone else!

Before Unit 1

Progress Check *Can I?*

After Unit 1

☐ Ask and answer questions to help me understand a story. ☐

☐ Retell important details to help determine a story's message. ☐

☐ Describe the characters and how their actions affect the story. ☐

☐ Use context clues in a sentence to learn the exact meaning of unknown words. ☐

HOME♦CONNECT...

Focused readers **ask and answer questions** as they read. What is the story about? Who are the characters? How does the story turn out? Finding important details to answer questions helps your child understand the meaning of a story. Choose a print or online text your child might enjoy. Read it together, asking each other questions such as "What's going to happen next?"

Knowing the author's **central message or lesson** in a story lets children relate the story to their own life. Choose a print or online folktale about a character you and your child admire. Take turns reading aloud to each other. Then ask questions such as "What can we learn from this character?" and "How would we act in a similar situation?"

Uncovering **characters' traits and motivations** helps young readers understand why things happen in a story. Why did the character do this? Watch a television drama with your child. During breaks, talk about what the characters said and did. Make predictions about the story's outcome based on your observations.

Conversation Starter: With your child, brainstorm what might occur if a hero from a myth or folktale were brought to life in the modern world. How would the character's powers or skills be used today? How would modern people react to the character? Sketch pictures of the original hero and how the character's appearance would change.

IN THIS UNIT, YOUR CHILD WILL...

- Ask questions and answer them, using details from the text, to gain a better understanding of the text as a whole.

- Retell stories, including important details about characters, setting, and events.

- Determine the central message of a text and how the author conveys the message through details.

- Describe characters' traits and motives and explain how their actions move a story along.

- Use context clues to define words that are unknown or that have multiple meanings.

- Compare and contrast three texts with the same theme: a fable, a folktale, and a myth.

NOTE: All of these learning goals are based on the Grade 3 Common Core State Standards for English Language Arts.

WAYS TO HELP YOUR CHILD

Help your child enjoy reading. Encourage your child to find and share short texts about interesting topics, and read them aloud to each other. Ask questions about the texts that promote reasoning skills: Why do you think the person did that? What might have been a better thing to do? Challenge your child to offer supporting reasons for any opinions.

ONLINE

For more Home Connect activities, continue online at sadlierconnect.com

Reading Literature: Key Ideas and Details

Essential Question:
How do authors convey a central message or lesson?

RL.3.1

WORDS TO KNOW

condition
hatchling
swooped

> To understand a text, **find details** in the text to help you **answer questions**.

CITE EVIDENCE

A To understand a story, it helps to **ask and answer questions**, such as, *What characters are in the story?* Underline details in the title that answer this question. It also helps to ask, *What is the main problem?* Circle the part of paragraph 2 that answers this.

B Questioning why characters do things is also important. Underline the sentences in paragraph 4 that explain why the Dove does what she does. What other fables or folktales have you read in which one character helps another?

The Dove and the Ant:
A Retelling of an Aesop Fable
(Genre: Fable)

1   The weather in the spring had been very hot and dry. An Ant dragged herself to the river, hoping to get a drink of water. However, weak from thirst, she fell into the water. As she struggled to get back to land, the current carried her away from shore.

2   Try as she might, the Ant could not get closer to shore. There was nothing else floating in the river for her to hold on to. "I am lost!" she thought. "Nobody saw me fall in. There is nobody to help me." Getting more and more tired, the Ant started to sink beneath the water.

3   High in a tree near the bank of the river sat a sharp-eyed Dove. Her strong eyes let her see the Ant splashing, and she knew the Ant was in trouble. She thought to herself, "What can I do?"

4   The Dove pitied the Ant's **condition**. She wanted to help. Spotting a small branch on the ground, she **swooped** down and grabbed it in her beak. She took a hop and flew out over the river.

5   Where was the Ant? The Dove saw the weakest of splashes. Zooming out of the sky, she dropped the branch right by the Ant.

6   The Ant felt the branch. She got one leg up on it, then another, and finally scrambled on top. She shook the water from her eyes. Seeing that the Ant was safe, the Dove flew away.

7   The branch floated to shore, and the Ant stepped off onto land. "I have to thank the Dove," she thought to herself. "I don't know how I will, but I have to."

8   Spring turned to summer. The Dove's **hatchlings** grew, and the young birds left the nest. The Dove forgot all about saving the Ant.

9   The Ant also had work to do. With her mates, she tunneled underground. She also searched for food above ground and brought it back to the nest.

CITE EVIDENCE

C Ask yourself, "What words does the author use that help me see the action?" Circle the words in paragraph 5 that help you see what is happening.

D The story's setting includes *when* it happens. Underline details that tell you when this story happens. How much time passes in this story?

Comprehension Check

1. Why does the Ant think she is in big trouble?

2. What in the text says that the Ant feels grateful?

ASKING AND ANSWERING QUESTIONS

The Dove and the Ant: A Retelling of an Aesop Fable *continued*

RL.3.1

WORDS TO KNOW

bait
commotion
stealthy

CITE EVIDENCE

A Ask yourself if the setting has changed. Underline the words in paragraph 11 that show that one part of the setting, the season, has changed.

B On page 15, circle two sentences where the Ant boldly helps the Dove. Think of a time when you took action to help a friend.

10   The Ant sometimes talked to her friends about the Dove. "Why worry about that? You will never be able to thank her," they said. "Now help me lift this blade of grass."

11   By the fall, hunters started coming into the woods. Some were noisy and would crash through the trees, wearing bright red and yellow coats. The animals had an easy time avoiding loud hunters.

12   Other hunters were **stealthy**. They walked quietly, and wore green and brown clothes. The bushes did not rustle as the quiet hunters went past. The animals had to be on the lookout for these hunters.

13   One day, the Ant was alone near a clearing in the woods. A young man was lying on his stomach at the edge of the opening, looking as if he was enjoying the fine weather. But the Ant did not like something about him. It wasn't just that he looked out of place there.

14   He had covered himself with leafy branches. He was holding two ropes in his hands, but he was not moving at all. And he was looking up into the branches of the tree above him.

15   The Ant understood. The ropes were a net, and the man had put **bait** in the net! The Ant looked up into the tree. Sitting on a branch eyeing the food on the ground was the Dove!

16   The Ant scrambled onto the man's hand. As she did, the Dove fluttered to the ground. The Ant had to hurry.

17   The Ant bit the man hard on the hand. The man yelled and slapped his hand. The Dove heard the **commotion** and hopped to safety. As the Dove flew away, the Ant thought, "I did it. I saved my friend!"

18   *Moral: Little friends may prove to be great friends.*

Comprehension Check

1. What is the young man in the story trying to do?

    a. get closer to the Dove to take her picture

    b. make friends with the Dove by giving her food

    c. rescue the Dove because it is injured

    d. trap the Dove, using food as bait

2. Why is the Ant so excited at the end of the fable?

    a. She defeated a much bigger enemy.

    b. She was able to save the Dove from danger.

    c. She can go back to her life without the Dove.

    d. She was able to drive the hunters out of the woods.

3. A moral tells the reader an important message of a fable. Think of questions you might ask and answer to prove that the moral given is correct. Use details from the story in your answers.

_____

_____

_____

_____

RL.3.1

WORDS TO KNOW

despair
grief
invention

CITE EVIDENCE

A Circle words in paragraphs 1 and 2 that tell where this fable happens.

B Why was it difficult to get water from the pitcher? Underline evidence from the text in your answer.

The Crow and the Pitcher:
A Retelling of an Aesop Fable
(Genre: Fable)

1   A Crow was faint with thirst. He was so thirsty that he was too weak to fly. The country road was so dusty that his beautiful black feathers turned gray. The dust got in his throat, making his need for water even greater.

2   As he passed a small farmhouse, the Crow could not believe what he saw. On the front porch stood a tall clay pitcher. It was the kind used to hold water. The Crow ran to it with delight. But when he reached it, his joy turned to **grief**. The pitcher contained only a little water.

3   He could not reach the water with his beak. If he turned the pitcher over, the water would run out. If he broke the pitcher, he would also lose the water. He had to have that water! He thought and thought until his head hurt.

4   In **despair**, he looked around at the pebbly ground. Pebbles! He picked up a few in his beak and dropped them in the pitcher. Again and again he did this. Soon the water level started to rise. At last the water was high enough that the Crow could reach it.

5   The pebbles and his own brainpower had saved the Crow's life.

6   *Moral: Necessity is the mother of* **invention**. *In other words, having a problem gives you a good reason to work hard toward a solution.*

Comprehension Check

(MORE ONLINE) **sadlierconnect.com**

1. Why is it so important for the Crow to get water?

   a. He is dying of thirst.

   b. He has to wash his feathers.

   c. He needs to rinse his throat to talk.

   d. He likes the pitcher.

2. According to the text, how does the Crow finally get the water?

   a. by finding a nearby stream

   b. by knocking over the pitcher

   c. by dropping pebbles in the pitcher

   d. by asking the owner of the farmhouse

3. Reread the moral at the end of this fable. Why do you think the author wrote this fable? Use information from the text in your answer.

_____

_____

_____

_____

DETERMINING A CENTRAL MESSAGE

RL.3.2

WORDS TO KNOW
cave-in
lay claim
steam-powered

To explain how a folktale **conveys its central message**, you can **retell the key details** of the story.

CITE EVIDENCE

A To understand the **central message** of the folktale, look for how the author uses **key details** to communicate the central message. In paragraphs 1–2, circle the details that tell whom the folktale is about.

B In paragraph 4, underline the key details that provide this folktale's setting—its time and place. Many stories take place long ago or in faraway places. What is the setting of one of your favorite stories?

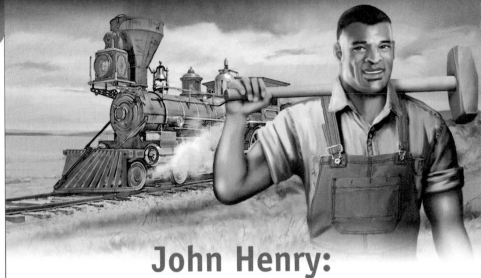

John Henry:
A Retelling of an American Folktale
(Genre: Folktale)

1   John Henry was a giant of a man. Some say he was born in Virginia. Some say Carolina or Alabama. It seems like every state wants to **lay claim** to John Henry.

2   It seems pretty certain that John Henry was a real steel-driving man. He was born into slavery in the 1840s but was freed after the Civil War. He found work as a steel-driver for the Chesapeake & Ohio Railroad. He was known as the most powerful man working the rails.

3   The work was dangerous and back-breaking. The men drilled holes in solid rock. It might take all day to drill holes deep enough for blasting. And the tunnel might advance only 10 feet a day!

4   In 1870, the C&O Railroad was being built through West Virginia. But right in its path was Big Bend Mountain. It was more than a mile through that mountain. The men of the C&O were going to drill right through the heart of it by hand.

RL.3.2

5   It took three long years to get through Big Bend. As many as a thousand workers lost their lives. If the **cave-ins** didn't get them, the smoke and dust did. Through it all, John Henry worked tirelessly. Some say he swung a 9-pound hammer. Some say it was 14 pounds or even 20 pounds! No other steel-driving man could match him for drilling holes.

6   The story is told that one day a salesman showed up at John Henry's camp. He had with him a **steam-powered** drill. He said it could outdrill any man. Those were fighting words to John Henry. They set up a contest: John Henry against the machine!

CITE EVIDENCE

C Folktales often include larger-than-life characters whose special abilities move the story toward its central message. In paragraph 5, circle John Henry's special abilities.

D A folktale's central message is often reached by way of a dramatic event or contest. Underline the event or contest agreed upon in paragraph 6.

Comprehension Check

How is John Henry different from the other workers on the C&O Railroad?

John Henry: A Retelling of an American Folktale *continued*

RL.3.2

WORDS TO KNOW

onlooker
outdrilled
spirit

CITE EVIDENCE

A A story sometimes gives clues about what might happen later in the story. Circle a clue in paragraph 7 about what might happen later.

B Underline the key detail in paragraph 10 that shows what happened to the hero. Was the price the hero paid worth what he had won?

7   Some men said John Henry couldn't beat the machine. Some said he was holding back the future. But according to one of the songs sung about him:
> *"John Henry said to the Captain,*
> *'A man ain't nothing but a man*
> *But before I let that steam drill drive me down*
> *I'll die with this hammer in my hand.'"*

8   The contest began. Pretty soon, the smoke and steam started to choke the **onlookers**. The noise of the drilling matched the noise of the cheering. John Henry drilled deeper into the mountain. The machine did the same.

9   Some say man and machine fought it out from sunup to sundown. Others say it took less than an hour. Some say John Henry swung two 20-pound hammers, one in each hand. But everyone agrees on the result. John Henry **outdrilled** that steam drill!

10   John Henry held up his hammers in triumph! The men shouted and cheered. But folks tell different stories about what happened next. John Henry was exhausted, and some say the great man fell to the ground, his hammers rolling away. The foreman rushed to his side. But it was too late. The greatest driller in the C&O Railroad gave his life to prove he was faster than the machine.

11   John Henry lives on in song and story. New tunnels are being dug every year. Workers risk their lives to go into the darkness to do their jobs. And with them goes the **spirit** of John Henry: a man who was nothing but a man.

Comprehension Check

1. According to the text, why is it hard to say how John Henry died?

   a. No one thought it was important.

   b. No one remembers how he died.

   c. People tell different stories about John Henry.

   d. He disappeared and no one ever saw him again.

2. What superhuman feat does John Henry do in the story?

   a. He lives for a very long time.

   b. He works as a steel-driving man.

   c. He outdrills a machine in a contest.

   d. He drills deeper holes than any other worker.

3. Almost 150 years have passed since John Henry's feat. Machines have taken over most drilling work. Why is the story of John Henry still retold? Cite information from the text to support your answer.

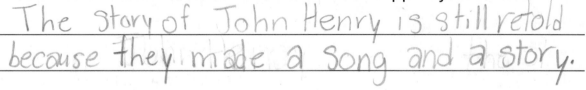

The story of John Henry is still retold because they made a song and a story.

DETERMINING A CENTRAL MESSAGE

Independent Practice

RL.3.2

WORDS TO KNOW
hinge
massive
ultimate

CITE EVIDENCE

A Underline the sentences in paragraph 1 that tell you unusual details about the main character in the story and his boat.

B In paragraph 5, circle a detail about Stormalong's battle with the giant octopus. Use this detail to tell how Stormalong and John Henry are alike.

Old Stormalong and the Octopus:
A Retelling of an American Folktale
(Genre: Folktale)

1   Old Stormalong was the **ultimate** sailor. He stood 30 feet tall, although he was only 12 feet tall when he was born. His sailing boat, the *Courser*, was built to his size. Its masts were on **hinges** so it could sail past the Moon without scraping it.

2   One day Stormalong told his crew to lift anchor. But the anchor was stuck on something! Try as they might, the crew could not get it unstuck. Even Stormalong couldn't pull it loose. So Stormalong decided to go down to the depths of the ocean to see what was tangling the anchor.

3   Taking only a knife, Stormalong dove into the water. Soon the waters below the **massive** ship began to bubble. The waves grew higher and higher until the ship was tossed around like a rubber duck. Finally the sea grew calm. But there was still no sign of the captain! As the crew was about to give up hope, Stormalong popped up on deck. "All's clear, boys. Hoist the anchor!" he shouted.

4   The crew gathered around Stormalong, shouting questions. "What was holding us? How did you get us loose? How did you save us and the ship?"

22

5   "It was a giant octopus, twice as big as me," Stormalong explained. "It had grabbed the anchor with four legs. It was holding on to the seafloor with the other four legs. So I arm-wrestled the beast, one arm at a time. After I beat the last arm, I tied all of them into knots." Stormalong shrugged. "It will take him a week to get himself undone." And off Old Stormalong sailed!

Comprehension Check
    (MORE ONLINE) sadlierconnect.com

1. Folktales use exaggeration to tell about the characters. What do the exaggerated details in the story tell you about Stormalong?

    a. He is able to sail anywhere he wants.

    b. He is unusually strong, brave, and determined.

    c. He has a strange sense of humor.

    d. He needs a crew of people to help him.

2. Exaggerated details in a folktale are often based on a real problem. What is MOST LIKELY real in the story?

    a. A sailor wrestling an octopus

    b. An anchor stuck on the sea bottom

    c. A sailor diving to the bottom of the ocean

    d. An octopus holding on to an anchor

3. In a few sentences, retell the story of how Stormalong freed the *Courser*. Then cite evidence to support the folktale's message.

Stormalong freed the Courser by taking a knife, but instead he tangled the giant octopuses legs.

Guided Instruction

RL.3.3

WORDS TO KNOW

approaching
expert
murmur
offering

Think about details that help you **understand characters** and why they do what they do.

CITE EVIDENCE

A Each **character** has **feelings, qualities,** or **motivations** that help explain how he or she acts. Underline the words in paragraph 1 that tell how the king is feeling.

B In paragraph 2, circle the sentence that explains why Artemis sent the boar. Folktales and myths often have fantastical creatures in them. Which other story in this unit features a giant creature?

Atalanta the Huntress
(Genre: Myth)

1   In troubled days, when the tribes were on the edge of war, King Oineus made **offerings** to the gods with a heavy heart. To the goddess of the harvest, he gave the first fruits of the field. To the god of grapes, he poured fine wine. To the goddess of wisdom, he offered shimmering oil from her sacred trees. To each god who dwells on Mount Olympus, the king gave what was fitting—except one. Full of worries, he forgot to offer flowers to Artemis, goddess of the hunt.

2   The goddess was offended. In anger, she sent a giant boar to the land around the city. The great boar ran wild. It tore up crops and farms. It chased the dogs and ruined the herds. It attacked farmers and travelers alike. Brave men did their best to put an end to the terror. They failed, one after another. The king was too old to go after the beast. And his good son, Meleager, was away on another adventure. Now the people were afraid. What was the king to do?

RL.3.3

3   The aged king did his best to comfort the people. He sent word for help across all of Greece. **Expert** hunters and grim soldiers answered the call. The king, however, waited for his son, Meleager, to return. At last, the watchmen at the city walls saw Meleager and his friends **approaching**. On his way to the city, the king's son had seen the ruined farms and empty homes. From tough farmers who wouldn't leave their places, he learned about the curse of Artemis upon the land. Now the king's brave son entered the city with his friends. The citizens cheered as the group of twenty men marched into town. Then a **murmur** broke through the crowd. The people saw among those hard fighters a beautiful young woman. It was the huntress, Atalanta.

CITE EVIDENCE

C Descriptive words, such as adjectives, help readers understand characters. Circle each adjective in paragraph 3 that describes a character.

D A story can only move forward through characters' actions. Underline the action of the new characters in the story. How do you think the arrival of Meleager and his friends will change the story?

The King forgot because he was worried. Artemis was angry, so she gave the city a giant boar.

Comprehension Check

Why did the king forget Artemis and what was the result of his forgetfulness? Cite text evidence in your answer.

DESCRIBING CHARACTERS

Atalanta the Huntress *continued*

RL.3.3

WORDS TO KNOW

Centaur
focused
outrage

CITE EVIDENCE

A Circle evidence in paragraph 4 that provides information about Atalanta's traits.

B Underline the sentences in paragraphs 5 and 6 that describe how Atalanta's arrival affects the events that follow.

4   People said a bear found Atalanta in the forest when she was a baby. The animal cared for Atalanta until a family of hunters found her. They raised her as their own in a wild mountain home. Atalanta grew up fit and strong. She learned to hunt and fight. She was as fine an archer as any man. She had a **focused**, steady eye. Everyone told stories about Atalanta. Two **Centaurs** once attacked the girl while she hunted in the forest. She heard them coming. She laid them low with two shafts from her bow. She once defeated the great wrestler Peleus in a fair match. She fought beside Meleager in far-off lands and didn't complain when she was injured.

5   Now here she was, traveling with the fierce friends of Meleager. Atalanta walked proudly among them. She was taller than many of the men. Her long hair was pulled back in a single braid. She carried a bow and a quiver of arrows over her shoulders. Whoever dared to meet her gaze saw a light that burned like fire in her eyes. The heroes got ready to hunt. The king came to meet them. People strained their necks for a glimpse of Atalanta.

26

6   In those dark, ancient days, it was strange to see a woman standing equal with such men. Women didn't hunt, or fight, or wrestle champions. When they realized Atalanta was joining the hunt, some of Greece's bravest heroes grew red in the face. A few reacted with **outrage**. They said they wouldn't hunt beside a woman. But Meleager asked, "Are you afraid you won't match up?" Since no one would admit this, the hunt was on.

Comprehension Check

1. According to the text, most of the people in the crowd probably want to see Atalanta because they are

   a. angry

   b. curious

   c. jealous

   d. hopeful

2. Which is a trait that is NOT supported by the text's description of Atalanta?

   a. brave

   b. unusual

   c. talented

   d. enthusiastic

3. Why were some of the heroes offended when they discovered Atalanta would be joining the hunt? Use evidence from the text to show the effects her actions had on following events.

   Atalanta is a brave woman because she did something very special to her.

DESCRIBING CHARACTERS

RL.3.3

WORDS TO KNOW
bloodshot
enormous
intervened

CITE EVIDENCE

A Circle evidence in paragraph 7 that suggests the boar is a supernatural, mythical creature.

B Underline where Meleager stands up to the men in support of Atalanta. This shows Meleager's loyalty to his friend. Is loyalty important to you and your friends?

Atalanta the Huntress *continued*

7   The heroes set out to find the trail. They found marks of hooves and tusks. They unleashed their dogs to track the beast by its scent. A long time passed before the trail led to a deep, rocky valley. Now the hunters heard the dogs' wild barking ahead. They sprang into action. Atalanta was the first to see the boar. Big as a bull, it stomped and charged to keep the dogs at bay. Its **bloodshot** eyes burned like red coals. Its long tusks were as sharp as spears. Sparks flew from its tusks and set the grass on fire.

8   Atalanta stood still as stone, waiting for a clear shot. Two running hunters cast a net to catch the **enormous** boar between them. The monster charged, taking both men to the ground. It ran off, dragging the net behind. The dogs blocked its path. Now thirty hunters took their places. Each spear thrown missed its mark, as if Artemis herself had **intervened**. The boar snorted fiercely. Men and dogs lay wounded on the ground, or limped away from danger. Atalanta took one shot and missed her target. Her second arrow struck the beast behind its ear. When the boar went wild, it was Meleager who brought it down with his long spear.

28

9   Back in the city, the old king offered the monster's hide to his son. Meleager said the trophy wasn't his. He gave it to the huntress, the first to hit the mark. Some of the men were outraged to see the honor go to a woman. When Meleager wouldn't budge, his own uncles stood to leave the city. They left with a promise: "You haven't heard the last from us."

Comprehension Check

MORE ONLINE   sadlierconnect.com

1. Which is a reason Meleager probably did NOT have for giving the trophy to Atalanta?

   a. He did not think she deserved it.

   b. He was grateful for Atalanta's help.

   c. He wanted to prove a point.

   d. Atalanta hit the boar first.

2. What character's (or characters') actions seem to protect the boar from the hunters?

   a. King Oineus

   b. the gods on Mount Olympus

   c. Artemis

   d. Meleager's uncles

3. What does the anger of Meleager's uncles make them promise, and what do they mean? Use details to support your answer.

Meleager's uncles mean you did not hear the last word yet.

Heracles and Atlas

(Genre: Myth)

1   When Zeus, king of gods, married Hera, the couple received a gift from Mother Earth. She gave them beautiful golden apples. These apples sparkled like the setting sun and brought joy to anyone who ate them. Hera planted them in the home of the Hesperides, three nymphs who were daughters of the Titan, Atlas. A garden of apple trees sprang up there. Hera asked the nymphs to protect the enchanted garden. She asked them to care for her fruit. But the nymphs couldn't help themselves from eating the apples—such sweet joy it was to eat them! So Hera brought a fierce dragon, Ladon, into the garden. The dragon would help the nymphs protect the garden from intruders. And it would help protect the apples from the nymphs.

2   Now the old Titan, Atlas, once made war against the king of gods. When he lost, Zeus banished him to the garden of the Hesperides. Then he lifted the dome of the Sky and put it on Atlas's shoulders. Now the Titan would stand forever, carrying the weight of the Sky in his daughters' garden.

3   Many years later, a king ordered Heracles to bring him apples from that garden. When the king commanded, Heracles obeyed. But there was one small problem. Nobody seemed to know how to find the garden of the Hesperides.

4   Heracles, a son of Zeus himself, set out to find it. He scoured the world, searching high and low. But he couldn't find the garden. Eventually, he decided to ask Atlas's brother, Prometheus. Maybe he would know where it was hidden. Prometheus was easy to track down. He was chained to a mountain. Zeus had bound him there years ago, to punish him for stealing fire from the gods. Heracles went to Prometheus and made him an offer. "You've suffered long enough for your crime. I'll break these chains and set you free. But first, promise to tell me where to find the garden of the Hesperides. I'm bound to get some apples there."

5   Prometheus agreed. Heracles took one heavy chain in each hand. His whole body straining, he broke the chains with one tug. In return, Prometheus told him where he could find the garden. It was hidden in the mountains at the western edge of the world. He gave the hero a warning. The dragon that guarded the apples was too powerful to defeat, even for a son of Zeus.

6   Following Prometheus's directions, Heracles found the mountain at the edge of the world. He climbed the rocky mountain until he reached a moss-covered ridge. On the other side he saw the garden of the Hesperides, full of trees. Green and yellow leaves whispered in the breeze. Apples shone like little setting suns. The whole garden glowed with their golden light. Under the trees, Heracles saw three nymphs singing. He could barely hear their voices, sweet as the apples they loved. Curled around them, at their feet, was the dragon, Ladon. The creature was blue, like a deep river. Its long tail encircled the garden. Steam hissed from its nostrils when it breathed.

7   Across the garden stood old Atlas, with his back to a rocky peak, holding up the Sky. How strong he was! How still he stood under his load! Quietly Heracles crept down to the spot where Atlas stood. He told Atlas how he was sent by a king to fetch the apples. And the hero made an offer. "You must be tired, old man, from carrying that load. I'll take it from you for a little while and give you some relief. But you must promise to bring me apples from your daughters' garden." Atlas had suffered so long under the heavy Sky. He was quick to agree.

8   Mighty Atlas grunted. Gently, he raised up the dome of the Sky. Heracles eased the burden off the Titan's shoulders. The hero groaned as the heavens pressed down on him. And for the first time in centuries, Atlas was free. The Titan heaved a massive sigh that shook the trees. He stretched himself. He kneeled to the ground. He laughed so hard he almost cried. Then, without a word, he bounded off to fetch the apples. Heracles strained under the weight of the Sky. He wondered how long he could hold it. He wondered if Atlas would ever return. For a moment he began to despair.

9   Soon Atlas returned with the apples. There was a crafty look in his eye as he spoke. "Too long I've suffered with that burden. I'm happy to be free. You're strong enough to hold it. In exchange, I'll do your duty. I'll bring these apples to your king." Heracles shuddered at these words. But he didn't lose his wits.

10   "You're right, old man. You've suffered long enough. But before you go, hold up this Sky one last time. I'm not as tough as you. I want to get some rags to cushion my poor shoulders." Atlas shrugged and laid the apples down. Once more he took his place beneath the Sky. Now it was Heracles's turn to laugh. "I'm sorry, friend, but I won't trade my fate for yours." He grabbed the golden apples and departed.

11   Heracles couldn't blame Atlas. The hero had shared the Titan's burden. He knew how Atlas felt. Years later, he returned to the garden of the Hesperides. There he built two enormous pillars, strong enough to support the heavens. Now the pillars did the work old Atlas had done for too long. So Atlas lived in peace in the garden. He guarded the pillars that Heracles built. And he no longer bore the weight of the Sky.

Comprehension Check

1. Which detail helps you answer the question: What is the main problem Heracles faces in the story?

   a. The three nymphs eat the golden apples.

   b. Heracles returns to rescue Atlas.

   c. Precious golden apples are protected in a secret garden.

   d. The garden glows with the light of the apples.

2. Why is Prometheus chained to a mountain, and why does Atlas hold up the sky?

   a. They stole apples from the garden of the Hesperides.

   b. They were being punished by Zeus, the king of gods.

   c. They wanted to prove they were strong.

   d. They wanted to trick Heracles.

3. In paragraph 8, Heracles takes the Sky off Atlas's shoulders. Provide at least three details from the text to describe how Atlas behaved once he was free. How does Heracles's action lead to the next event in the myth?

Atlas behaved like he was centuries, he put his knee to the ground and started laugh, and to cry, he bounded off a fetch the apples.

4. Why did Heracles return to the garden to build pillars for Atlas? Use evidence from the text to support your answer.

Heracles return to the garden to build pilles because he wanted to get the golden apples.

RL.9, SL.3.1.a, SL.3.1.c, SL.3.1.d, SL.3.4

Compare and Contrast Texts

In this unit, you read about the Dove and the Ant, the Crow, John Henry, Stormalong, Atalanta, and Heracles and Atlas. Think about the characters in these stories. Then choose any two characters and compare and contrast them, using the T-chart below. List key details and other evidence from the texts to show similarities and differences. Be prepared to discuss your ideas with the class.

Similarities	Differences

Return to the Essential Question

How do authors convey a central message or lesson?

In small groups or as a class, discuss the Essential Question. Think about what you have learned about asking and answering questions, identifying details and determining the central message of a text, and describing characters. Use evidence from the six unit texts to answer the question.

Context Clues

L.3.4.a

> **bound 1.** *(adj.)* going or ready to go: She is **bound** for home. **2.** *(n.)* a leap or jump: They crossed the field in leaps and **bounds**.

Guided Instruction **Context clues** can help you understand the meanings of unknown and multiple-meaning words. After using context clues, you can check the meanings in a dictionary.

Read this sentence from "Heracles and Atlas": *I'm bound to get some apples there*. Context clues in the text indicate that this sentence uses meaning 1 of *bound*.

Look at the chart to find other examples of multiple-meaning words.

track	1. *(n.)* a course for running 2. *(v.)* to follow the tracks of
scour	1. *(v.)* to clean by rubbing 2. *(v.)* to move quickly while searching

Guided Practice Write the number of the meaning of the word from the chart above that appears in each sentence.

_(n.)_ **1.** The hunter learned to *track* animals in the forest.

_(v.)_ **2.** Bring your sneakers if you're going to the *track*.

_(v.)_ **3.** Will you *scour* this sticky pot with this kitchen sponge?

_(v.)_ **4.** I'll *scour* the city until I find her.

Independent Practice Write the correct meanings of the word in italics. Use context clues and a dictionary to help you.

How long do you think the game will *last*?

last means to continue in time.

The shoemaker used his tools to *bore* a hole in leather.

Bore means to make hole with a tool.

RL.3.1, RL.3.2, RL.3.3, L.3.4.a

Read the following passage in which you can apply skills for asking and answering questions, identifying details and determining the central message, and understanding characters. Then answer the questions on pages 37 and 38.

The Daydreamer

(Genre: Folktale)

1   A poor farmer was walking through his fields, when he saw a rabbit hopping a few feet ahead.

2   "What a stroke of luck!" he shouted. "I'll catch that rabbit. I'll sell it at the market for ten dollars. With the money I earn, I'll buy a fat pig. The pig will have piglets. The piglets will grow to be big as their mother. Soon I'll be rich!

3   "I'll hire a housekeeper and cook. I'll get married. My wife will have two sons, Ilya and Ivan. The boys will plow the fields when they're able. I'll sit on the porch and supervise.

4   "'Hey boys,' I'll holler. 'Ilya and Ivan! Don't work yourselves too hard! You know you were born stinking rich!'"

5   The farmer bellowed these last words so loud that the rabbit was frightened and fled. So his riches, his wife, and his children were lost.

Fill in the circle of the correct answer choice.

1. Because the farmer is daydreaming, the rabbit

   ○ is caught

   ○ is sold

   ◉ escapes

   ○ bellows

2. *Bellowed* is closest in meaning to

   ○ daydreamed

   ○ whispered

   ○ listened

   ◉ shouted

3. The farmer's wife

   ○ cooks and cleans

   ◐ has two sons

   ● does not exist

   ○ scolds him

4. The farmer is best described as

   ○ hard-working

   ◐ capable

   ○ angry

   ● foolish

5. Underline the phrase *stroke of luck* in paragraph 2, sentence 1. Explain the meaning of this phrase in your own words.

   Stroke of luck means that he/she is lucky.

6. Underline the word *supervise* at the end of paragraph 3. Provide the meaning of this word below.

   Supervise means I will look and be in charge.

7. What did the farmer think the rabbit would bring him?

   The farmer think the rabbt that it would make him get rich.

8. What is the central message of this story?

   The central message of the story is to work hard and not be foolish.

9. How do the farmer's actions show what he was like?

   The farmer's actions was loud because he was shouting, and made the rabbit run off, he is a foolish person aswell.

10. What lesson should the farmer learn based on story events?

    The farmer should learn that if he worked hard to get what he wants. and lose your wishes.

Introducing UNIT 2

In this unit about animals, you will learn how to write a fictional narrative. A fictional narrative is a story about imaginary characters and events.

When you write a fictional narrative, you want to think carefully about the event sequence. The story should have a beginning, a middle, and an end. As a writer, you should help the reader by using words such as *first* and *then* to make the order clear.

To be effective, a fictional narrative should have carefully chosen words. The writer should use descriptive details and dialogue to help the reader understand the characters and events.

Before Unit 2

Progress Check   *Can I?*

After Unit 2

☐ ☐ Write a story with imaginary characters and events.

☐ ☐ Write the story with a beginning, middle, and end.

☐ ☐ Use dialogue and descriptive details.

☐ ☐ Use words to make the order of events clear.

☐ ☐ Choose words and phrases for effect.

☐ ☐ Write using nouns, including abstract nouns.

☐ ☐ Write using regular and irregular plural nouns.

☐ ☐ Write using possessives.

☐ ☐ Write using correct punctuation in dialogue.

In this unit, children will learn about writing **fictional narratives**. A fictional narrative tells about an imagined experience or events. After reading a fictional narrative with your child, ask him or her to retell the story. Point out that the story is told in **sequence** with a beginning, a middle, and an end. Encourage your child's writing imagination by asking what he or she might have changed about a story's events.

Invite your child to share the story that he or she writes for this unit. Ask questions about the **characters** and **narrators**, and decide together what you learn about the characters through what they say and do.

When writing narratives, writers choose precise words to **describe events** and show **how the characters think, feel, or act**. Encourage your child to concentrate on finding the best, most appropriate words and phrases in his or her writing. Ask your child what different words he or she might use in a passage of **description** or **dialogue** that the two of you read together.

Activity: Brainstorm about a character with your child. The character should be fictional but might be based on a real person you both know. Create a time and place for the character. With your child, describe how the character feels about something at a certain point (for example, lonely or excited). Then have your child write a few sentences of dialogue or description to show how the character feels.

IN THIS UNIT, YOUR CHILD WILL...

- Learn to write a story with imaginary characters and events, using dialogue, descriptive details, and a clear sequence of events.

- Learn to use linking words, such as *first, then,* and *finally* to signal the order of events.

- Learn language skills to use in writing a fictional narrative.

  - Recognize abstract nouns and use them in sentences.

  - Use the correct forms of regular and irregular plural nouns, such as *children* and *women*.

  - Use a possessive to show ownership, such as *Katie's skate*.

  - Write dialogue and use correct punctuation to show who is speaking.

NOTE: All of these learning goals for your child are based on the Grade 3 Common Core State Standards for English Language Arts.

WAYS TO HELP YOUR CHILD

Help your child to read like a writer. As your child reads, ask questions about the characters, such as *How does the writer show how the character feels?* or *Why do you think the writer included that event?* Emphasize that the writer thinks carefully about his or her word choice to help the reader understand the characters, actions, and settings.

ONLINE

For more Home Connect activities, continue online at sadlierconnect.com

Text Types and Purposes: Write Fictional Narratives

Essential Question:
How do writers develop fictional narratives?

W.3.3.a

CREATING AN ORGANIZATIONAL STRUCTURE

Drew used an outline to organize his **fictional narrative**. It is divided into three sections: beginning, middle, and end.

Title: _____
Setting: _____
Characters: _____
_____

I. Beginning
    Story Events
    _____
    _____

II. Middle
    Story Events
    _____
    _____

III. End
    Conclusion
    _____
    _____

EVENT SEQUENCE

- The beginning of the story gives information about the events and introduces the characters.

Underline the names of the characters on this page. Circle the event that happened last night.

Read a Student Model

Drew is a student in Mr. Tran's 3rd-grade class. He is writing a fictional narrative. He has been asked to use a clear event sequence and to use dialogue and descriptive details. As you read his story, think about how you will organize your fictional narrative.

What a Mess!

"Hoo-hoo, hoo-hoo!" Owl's voice was the signal that all was safe. Rabbit peeked from under the brush and hopped out into the opening. She jumped over a couple of fallen trees. As she looked around, other animals gathered.

Everyone was talking about the terrible storm that blew through last night. As Rabbit waited for the meeting to begin, she looked at the playground. It was covered with large branches, and trash was scattered everywhere. The broken swings hung limply. Just yesterday, the playground had been filled with laughter and joy. Now, it was a mess.

W.3.3.b, W.3.3.c

(Soon,) Tabby Cat's soft meow got everyone's attention. "Last night was a scary night." Some of the animals shivered thinking about the powerful winds that knocked down many trees. "Luckily," she continued, "we're all safe."

("Then) why did you bring us here?" wondered Mouse.

"I've been thinking of the children," Tabby Cat responded. "They will be so sad not to be able to play tomorrow."

The animals enjoyed watching the children run outside each day, eager to climb the monkey bars, swing with their friends, and race down the slides. The animals' bodies sagged with disappointment.

(At first), no one said anything. Then, Rabbit softly sighed. "We have to do something to help them."

(Next), Mouse looked around. "But what can we do? We are all so small, and the job is so big."

Everyone was quiet after that.

(Finally,) Brown Dog raised his head. "Well, I can fetch sticks!" He ran and picked up a few sticks, carrying them back.

Tabby Cat purred, "Well that's a start!" Rabbit looked at Tabby Cat and Brown Dog curiously. (Then) she [excitedly] hopped away. She picked up a piece of trash and put it with the sticks. (Soon,) the other animals began to cheer up. (Now,) they had a plan!

DIALOGUE

Dialogue shows thoughts and feelings of characters. Dialogue is surrounded by quotation marks.

Underline what Tabby Cat says that tells what she thinks about the children.

SEQUENCE WORDS

Use words and phrases to signal event order and make the event sequence clear.

Circle words that show the sequence of events.

DESCRIPTIONS OF ACTIONS, THOUGHTS, FEELINGS

Use descriptions to show how characters respond to events. Words such as *shivered* and *softly* help show characters' responses.

Box words in the last paragraph that show how Rabbit responds to Brown Dog's actions.

W.3.3.d

EVENT SEQUENCE

The ending completes the story for the reader. It shows how the problem is solved.

Underline the lesson the animals learn in the end.

Throughout the night, they worked. Mouse ran back and forth carrying bits of trash to the trash can. Owl and Hawk used their beaks to hang the swing back up. All the animals did what they could.

As the sun rose in the morning, Rabbit looked around once again. "I can't believe it!" she cheered. "The children will be so happy."

Mouse patted Rabbit on the back. "I thought the job was too big, but we did it!"

Tabby Cat smiled. "It's just like I always tell my kittens. Even the biggest jobs can be done when we all work together."

HW

W.3.3.a–d, W.3.4, W.3.5, W.3.10

Use an outline like the one below to organize your own fictional narrative about animal characters. Then write a first draft of your story on a separate sheet of paper. In your draft, be sure to use dialogue and descriptions of characters' thoughts, feelings, and actions to develop your story. Also, use words and phrases that clearly show your story's order of events. Finally, be sure to provide a clear ending. You will use this draft to write your final story draft in the Common Core Review section on page 52.

Title: What A Panda Day!

Setting: Panny's room, The Dining room.

Characters: Panny, mom, dad, little sister (little panda)

I. **Beginning**
   Story Events

   Panny was sleeping, Panny did not notice little panda was sheking through her room.

II. **Middle**
   Story Events

   Little panda mess up her room because she was mad last night, Panny stole her favorite toy.

III. **End**
   Conclusion

   When Panny woke up she went sceaming! Mom rushed to her room and said "what happend!? OMG! What did you do! with a mad face. I did'nt do anything Panny said. Mom said "You have to clean up your room NOW so I had to clean my room but I did not do anything.

L.3.1.a, L.3.1.c

Nouns

Guided Instruction A **noun** is a word that names a person, a place, or a thing. An **abstract noun** names something we cannot see or hold, such as *peace* or *talent*.

*I took my **dog** to the **park**.*
*My **brother** brought a **leash** and **water**.*
*A **pet** brings us great **joy**.*

Guided Practice Write *person*, *place*, or *thing* to tell what the underlined noun names. If it is an abstract noun, write *abstract*.

1. Drew got a new puppy yesterday. _thing_

2. He went to the store to get dog food and a leash. _place_

3. Mom and Drew took the puppy to see a vet. _person_

4. She needed treatment for one small problem. _abstract_

5. After the visit, they took the puppy to their house to rest. _place_

Independent Practice Use each abstract noun in a sentence.

1. childhood
   My dog was my best friend, when I was in my childhood.

2. friendship
   I have a great friendship is Eden and Angela.

3. courage
   I am courage when I dive in the pool.

L.3.1.b

Regular and Irregular Plural Nouns

Guided Instruction A **plural noun** names more than one person, place, or thing.

For most nouns, add the letter *s* to the end of the word.	For words ending in *s*, *ch*, *sh*, or *x*, add an *es* to the end of the word.	For some nouns that end in a consonant and *y*, change the *y* to an *i* and add *es*.
rabbit rabbits	*grass grasses* *lunch lunches* *box boxes*	*bunny bunnies*

Some nouns are irregular plurals. They do not end with the letter *s*. Instead, the spelling of the word is changed, or the word stays the same.

singular: man   mouse   deer
plural: men   mice   deer

Guided Practice Write the plural form of each word.

1. puppy _____puppies ✓_____
2. fox _____foxes ✓_____
3. hamster _____hamsters ✓_____
4. goose _____geese_____

Independent Practice Write the plural form of each word in parentheses to complete each sentence.

1. The _____children_____ learned how animals change. (child)
2. Caterpillars change into _____butterflies_____. (butterfly)
3. _____Birds_____ hatch from eggs. (Bird)

Possessives

Guided Instruction **Possessive** nouns show ownership. They show who has or owns something.

> The **horse that Sandeep owns** is at the fair.
> Possessive: **Sandeep's horse** is at the fair.

To form a singular possessive, add an apostrophe and the letter *s* to the end of the noun. To form a plural possessive to a word that ends with the letter *s*, add only an apostrophe at the end of the word.

> The **horse's** coat needs brushing. (singular possessive)
> The **horses'** gate was left open, and they ran out.
> (plural possessive)

Guided Practice Circle the phrase that is the correct possessive form.

1. the saddle that Tran has   (Tran's saddle)   Trans' saddle

2. the colts who have a mother   the colt's mother   (the colts' mother)

3. the stable of the horse   (the horse's stable)   the horses' stable

4. the spurs the riders have   (the riders' spurs)   the riders spurs'

Independent Practice Write the correct possessive form of the noun in parentheses to complete each sentence.

1. The horses ran in the ____farmer's____ field each day. (farmer)

2. They ate the ____meadow's____ grass. (meadow)

3. They listened for the ____boys'____ call to return to the barn. (boys)

4. The ____horses'____ lives were safe and enjoyable. (horses)

Commas and Quotation Marks in Dialogue

Guided Instruction **Dialogue** is a conversation written as part of a story.

> *Abbey said, "I would like a pet hamster."*

Quotation marks are used to show the person's words. A **comma** is used to separate the other words in the sentence from what the speaker says.

> *Mom asked, "Would you take care of the pet?"*

Guided Practice Add quotation marks to show each speaker's words.

1. Ryan asked, Do you have any guinea pigs?

   Ryan asked, "Do you have any guinea pigs"?

2. The owner answered, Yes. We have three.

   The owner answerd, "Yes. We have three."

3. That brown one sure is cute, Ryan whispered to his mom.

   "That brown one sure is cute" Ryan wispered his mom.

Independent Practice Write the sentence using quotation marks and commas to separate the speaker's words from the rest of the sentence.

1. Ben exclaimed The guinea pig doesn't look like a pig at all!

   Ben exclamed, The guinea pig doesn't look like a pig at all"!

2. How big do guinea pigs get? asked Katie.

   "How big do guinea pigs get?," asked Katie

3. Mrs. Volpe answered Adults are about two pounds.

   Mrs. Volpe answered, "Adults are about two pounds

SL.3.1.a–d, SL.3.3

Discuss the Essential Question

How do writers develop fictional narratives?

Think about the Essential Question by responding to the questions below. Support your point of view with reasons and experience.

1. How does the writer sequence the story?

First, the animals see the playground messy. Then, they all cleaned it up!

2. What are some words or phrases the author uses to describe events?

For example: The Auther uses fraxen like broken swings hung limply powerful and jagged with dissapoment.

Use your notes above to discuss the Essential Question in small groups or as a class. Remember to use the rules for being a good speaker and a good listener in the checklist below. When you speak, be sure to explain your ideas fully. As a listener, ask questions and make connections among everyone's comments in order to fully understand the conversation.

Did I:

- [ ] Come to the discussion prepared?
- [ ] Follow agreed-upon rules for discussion?
- [ ] Ask questions to check my understanding?
- [ ] Stay on topic?
- [ ] Avoid interrupting others?
- [ ] Listen carefully to others and answer questions?
- [ ] Speak in complete sentences?

L.3.1.a–c, L.3.2.c, L.3.2.d

This paragraph has mistakes in sentences and agreement. There are incorrect plural nouns and possessive forms, as well as incorrect punctuation of dialogue. Write the paragraph correctly on the lines below.

Lauren has two bunnys, Patches and Hopper. They were in a terrible flood. When the flood came, Lauren put them in boxs and carried them to safety. Lauren whispered You will be okay. Hearing her voice made them feel calm. Patches and Hopper didn't have their favorite grassies, but they did have plenty of water and food. After the flood, Laurens mom suggested that she teach other peoples how to help animals in emergencys.

Lauren has two bunnys, Patches and Hopper. They were in a terrible flood. When the flood came, Luaren put them in boxes an carried them safety. Luaren wispered, "You will be okay." Hearing her voice made them feel calm. Patches and Hopper didn't have their favorite grasses, but they did have plenty of water and food. After the flood, Lauren's mom suggested that she teach other people how to help aniabs in emergencies.

W.3.3.a–d, W.3.4, W.3.5, W.3.10

Assignment: Write a fictional narrative about animal characters.

On the lines below, write your final copy of the fictional narrative draft you created on page 45. Be sure to include dialogue and description to show thoughts, feelings, and actions. Make sure to choose your words carefully and use words to signal the order of events. Include a conclusion that wraps up events in your story. See the Writing Handbook (pages 275–283) for ways to improve your writing as you revise.

_____

_____

_____

_____

_____

_____

_____

_____

_____

_____

_____

_____

_____

_____

_____

Introducing UNIT 3

Human history, whether it is 50 years or 50,000 years ago, fascinates many people. Human beings are naturally social. They want to be connected to others—even others from our ancient past. This connectedness can help people of today in many ways.

In this unit, you will read about long-ago events. The echoes of these events still reach us today. The readings will show you people's desire to know the facts about our world. And they will explore how people use those facts to improve the present and the future. You will learn how authors craft informational texts to give readers a clear understanding of events and ideas. And you will also look at how authors use different words to express their exact meaning.

Being able to find and connect main ideas and details in texts will help you understand informational writing. This skill will help you understand your world.

Before Unit 3 ↓

Progress Check Can I? **After Unit 3** ↓

- ☐ Ask and answer questions about a text to better understand it. ☐
- ☐ Retell a text's important details to show understanding. ☐
- ☐ Summarize the main idea of a text. ☐
- ☐ Describe how events or ideas in a text are related. ☐
- ☐ Explain how certain words are used to describe real life. ☐

HOME ✦ CONNECT...

It is easy to **ask and answer questions** about a nonfiction text because it is full of details. Sometimes, asking yourself about what you have read is the only way to keep the information straight in your head. Choose a print or online news report on a topic of interest to your child. Use the article's title and subheadings to preview the subject and **main idea**. Read it together, asking and answering questions about **interesting details**. Pause at certain points to have your child summarize the information. Discuss the main idea of the text when you are done reading.

Authors of nonfiction texts use wording that **describes how a series of historical events or ideas are related**. In this unit, your child will learn about several important archaeological discoveries. Have your child describe events in his or her life that led to some kind of understanding or discovery. How did he or she come to play a certain sport, learn a new skill, or meet someone new? Talk together using language that connects different events.

On the Go: The texts in this unit focus on scientific research on ancient objects. With your child, think of ways that research skills might be used closer to your time and place. You might try to find out more about your ancestors, for example. Or, perhaps there is an old monument or landmark near your home. Finding out who built it and why can open up your town's history. A visit to a local historical society can add a hands-on element to any Internet research that you do.

IN THIS UNIT, YOUR CHILD WILL...

- Ask questions and answer them to gain a better understanding of an informational text.

- Determine the main idea of a text, and explain how details in the text support the main idea.

- Describe relationships between events or ideas in a text using words and phrases that show time order, sequence, and cause and effect.

- Connect the meaning of words to real-life situations.

- Compare and contrast four texts on the same theme: a magazine article, an historical text, a scientific text, and a biography.

NOTE: All of these learning goals for your child are based on the Grade 3 Common Core State Standards for English Language Arts.

WAYS TO HELP YOUR CHILD

Help your child connect "school" reading with everyday reading. Pick a topic from your child's schoolwork as a jumping off point. Use keywords from the topic to fuel an Internet search for similar, age-appropriate articles. Ask your child to tell you the most interesting facts from the articles. Follow up with your own search for additional information, either online or in print. Suggest that your child find out more about the subject and then teach you something new.

> (**ONLINE**)
> **For more Home Connect activities, continue online at** sadlierconnect.com

Reading Informational Text: Key Ideas and Details

Essential Question:
How do authors convey a main idea and use details to support it?

Guided Instruction

RI.3.1

WORDS TO KNOW

extinct
mammoth
prehistoric
sandbar

To **understand a text,** use details from the text **to ask and answer questions**.

CITE EVIDENCE

A To **understand a text**, it helps **to ask and answer questions**, such as *Who and what is the text about?* Underline details in paragraphs 1 and 2 that answer this question.

B It also helps to ask *What happened?* and *When did it happen?* Circle details in paragraph 2 that answer these questions. What other details give an idea of what happened next?

The 40,000-Year-Old Baby

by Hong Lee-Hyun

(Genre: Magazine Article)

1   Can long-**extinct** animals be brought back to life? The idea sounds like something out of a comic book. But a discovery in 2007 may have changed that.

2   In May 2007, Yuri Khudi was tending his herd of reindeer. He and his sons were near the Yuribey River. This river is in Siberia, in northeast Russia. They saw the body of a small animal lying on a **sandbar**. They could tell it was an animal they had never seen before.

3   They had heard of it, however. Their elders told many stories about the *mamonts*, or **mammoths**. These were giant beasts, like elephants. They were said to wander the frozen underworld. Yuri himself had seen many giant tusks. They came out of the frozen ground when spring arrived.

4   Yuri did not touch the body. According to his people, mammoths were bad luck. Instead, he traveled 150 miles south to the nearest museum. His story interested the museum director. He sent officials to recover the body.

5   When scientists looked at the body, they agreed with Yuri. It was a baby female mammoth. She was about three feet tall. She weighed 110 pounds. Being buried in the frozen soil of northern Russia had preserved her. They decided to name her Lyuba, after Yuri's wife.

6   Mammoths were **prehistoric** relatives of elephants. They were about the same size as elephants. They grew huge tusks and had long snouts, too. And they ate the same kinds of foods. But mammoths were able to live in very cold places. Their bodies were covered with a dense coat of long hair. They had small, fur-lined ears.

7   About 14,000 years ago, the mammoths started dying off quickly. Researchers argue about why. Most think a number of things combined to make them extinct. One cause was a general warming of Earth. Another may have been a disease. A third may have been overhunting by humans.

CITE EVIDENCE

C In most informational texts, it helps to ask *where* events happened. Box the words in paragraph 5 that answer this question.

D Texts that tell facts will also explain *why* something happened. Underline the details in paragraph 7 that tell why the mammoths died off. How can studying the reasons something in the past happened help scientists today?

Adult and baby mammoth

Comprehension Check

What animal that is alive today is like the mammoth? How are they alike and different? Use details from the text as a basis for your answer.

ASKING AND ANSWERING QUESTIONS

Guided Practice

RI.3.1

WORDS TO KNOW
biology
digestive system
skeleton

CITE EVIDENCE

A Check understanding by asking yourself *Who are the key people in this article?* Underline the name of each scientist on this page.

B Lyuba was an important discovery. In paragraph 9, circle the sentences that explain why. As you read, ask, *Why would the animal's stomach contents be important?*

The 40,000-Year-Old Baby *continued*

8   One of the first scientists to see Lyuba was Alexei Tikhonov. He was director of the St. Petersburg Zoological Museum in Russia. In July 2007, he called Dan Fisher at the University of Michigan. Fisher is an expert on prehistoric animals such as mammoths. When Fisher saw Lyuba, he was surprised and happy. This was the first time a prehistoric animal had been found in perfect shape!

9   Fisher knew what this find meant. Before, scientists could only imagine what the mammoths looked like. They only had **skeletons** or small body parts to look at. Now they had a fully formed mammoth! She looked as if she had been in good health when she died. Researchers could study her teeth and tusks. They could check her stomach contents and other features. These would reveal new facts on mammoth **biology** and habits.

10   To do these studies, Lyuba had to travel around the world. First, samples of her skin were sent to the Netherlands. There, they were tested to find out how long ago Lyuba lived. The tests showed that she had lived about 40,000 years ago. Next, in December 2007, Lyuba traveled to Japan. There, Naoki Suzuki performed detailed X-ray scans on her.

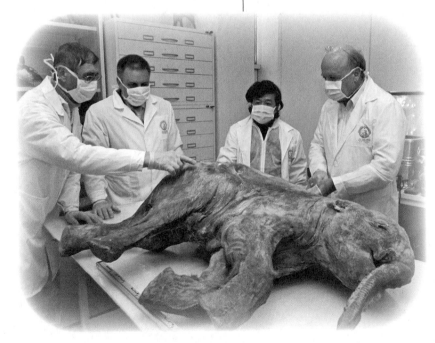

11   In June 2008, Fisher, Suzuki, and other scientists performed surgery on Lyuba. Some of them removed the contents of her **digestive system**. This finding told them about Lyuba's diet. Others drilled into a hump on her back. They took out fat to study. Suzuki inserted a tube into her body. He checked an area he had seen in the X-ray. Fisher took out some teeth and a tusk that was forming. Other samples of body parts were taken for further study.

Comprehension Check

1. Who is the main subject of this text?

   a. Lyuba, a baby mammoth

   b. Dan Fisher, an American scientist

   c. Alexei Tikhonov, a Russian scientist

   d. Yuri Khudi, a Russian reindeer herder

2. What happens to Lyuba after she is discovered?

   a. She is sent to a museum in Michigan.

   b. She is put on display in St. Petersburg, Russia.

   c. She is sold to a collector of prehistoric animals.

   d. She is studied by scientists from around the world.

3. Why is Lyuba so important to scientists who study extinct, prehistoric animals? Cite information from the text in your answer.

   Lyuba is the first mammath in good conducion.

Independent Practice

The 40,000-Year-Old Baby *continued*

RI.3.1

WORDS TO KNOW

cloning
DNA
exhibit
protein

CITE EVIDENCE

A Ask yourself *Why would surgery on a mammoth that was already dead need to be done quickly?* Circle details in paragraph 12 that answers this question.

B Underline details that tell about Lyuba's future. What questions about cloning Lyuba would you ask a scientist?

12 All the work had to be done in only three days. Before then, scientists kept Lyuba frozen. But for the surgery to happen, they had to warm her up. The scientists could not stop to figure out what their findings meant. They had to cut fast and think later.

13 When asked about those days, Fisher remembered the whirl of activity. There were things he noticed about Lyuba that did not make sense. It wasn't until later that he could reflect on what he had seen.

14 Since her surgery, Lyuba's travels have continued. In 2010, she became part of an **exhibit** at Chicago's Field Museum. The director of the exhibit was Professor Fisher. He was still studying Lyuba. He wanted to better understand how mammoths lived. The exhibit will continue traveling to museums around the world. Its final stop will be London in 2014.

15 Fisher was asked about **cloning** Lyuba. This process would mean using **DNA proteins** from Lyuba to create a new mammoth. He explains that DNA could be taken from Lyuba. However, he thought scientists were not close to being able to create a mammoth.

16 Other researchers think cloning Lyuba is possible sooner. In 2012, Russian and South Korean scientists agreed to work together on cloning. The South Koreans have already cloned a cat, dogs, a pig, a cow, and a wolf. They say they can produce a mammoth by 2015.

17   How is that possible? We already have elephants, which are distant relatives of mammoths. The scientists hope an elephant will be the cloned mammoth's mother. If they succeed, it would be one of the great moments in the history of science.

Comprehension Check   MORE ONLINE sadlierconnect.com

1. What did scientists have to do to perform surgery on Lyuba?

   a. take her to Chicago's Field Museum

   b. let her warm up

   c. create a new mammoth through cloning

   d. examine Lyuba's DNA proteins

2. In 2010, three years after her discovery, why was Professor Fisher still studying Lyuba?

   a. He wanted to better understand how mammoths lived.

   b. He wanted to extract DNA from Lyuba.

   c. He was the director of an exhibit in London.

   d. He had agreed to work on a project to clone Lyuba.

3. How would scientists clone Lyuba? Why are some scientists sure they can do this? By what date? Use information directly from the text in your answer.

   Scientist clone Lyuba by DNA proteins. Some sloths dogs, pigs, and cats. The date they want to able being to create a mammoth. The date was 2,14.

Guided Instruction

RI.3.2

WORDS TO KNOW
culture
ruins
tomb

Look for the **main idea** of a text. Find **key details** and explain how they **support the main idea**.

CITE EVIDENCE

A In an informational text, **details** in the title can point toward the **main idea**. In the title, draw a circle around three words that tell the main focus of this text.

B The author usually tells the reader the main idea early in the text. In paragraph 2, underline the sentence that tells the main idea. Why do scientists study things from long ago?

The Amazing Tomb of Tut

(Genre: Historical Text)

1   Howard Carter was a British scientist. He studied old cultures by digging up their **ruins**. He was very interested in Egypt. Its **culture** was thousands of years old. Ancient Egyptians made the pyramids and the Sphinx.

2   In 1922, Carter was digging in a part of Egypt called the Valley of the Kings. He had been working there for five years. Many Egyptian kings and queens were buried there thousands of years ago. Carter was searching for undiscovered **tombs**. He would soon find an amazing and important tomb.

Who Was King Tut?

3   Tutankhamun became pharaoh, or king, about 3,300 years ago. His name means "living image of the god Amun." We often call him "King Tut." During the time of his rule, Egyptians believed their kings were gods.

RI.3.2

4   Tut started his rule when he was nine years old. This was a difficult time in Egypt. Tut's father had made many changes in Egypt. He changed how the empire was run. He had forced Egyptians to change their religion. Many Egyptians were unhappy with what he did.

5   When Tut took the throne, he turned back his father's changes. After that, we know almost nothing about his rule. He was in poor health and died at the age of 19. Most of the facts about his rule were wiped out by the next rulers. Tut and his tomb were forgotten.

Life After Death

6   Egyptians believed in life after death. They built huge tombs for their rulers. The tombs took a long time to build. Sometimes work went on for the ruler's entire life.

7   Rulers and their subjects filled the tombs with things they thought the dead needed. These items included gold, jewelry, and furniture. People also thought the dead needed supplies for daily living. So they included spices, grains, and clothing.

8   Because Tut ruled for only 10 years, his tomb was not ready. He was buried in a tomb meant for another person. The entryway was covered by stones and dirt from other buildings.

A wall painting inside Tut's tomb

CITE EVIDENCE

C Authors include details that support the main idea of the text. In paragraph 5, underline important details about King Tut.

D Authors also explain things so readers can understand the main idea. In paragraphs 6 and 7, circle details about Egyptian life that readers need to know. How do these details help you understand Tut's world?

Comprehension Check

What details from the text help the reader understand why King Tut and his tomb were most likely forgotten?

Guided Practice

RI.3.2

WORDS TO KNOW

chamber
mummy
royal
sarcophagus

CITE EVIDENCE

A In this section, the author uses time order to provide details about finding the tomb. In paragraphs 10 and 11, circle words that show time passing as the details unfold.

B The author gives a step-by-step account of the discovery of the tomb. In paragraphs 11 and 12, underline the details that tell about this. How do these details support the main idea?

The Amazing Tomb of Tut *continued*

9   Over the years, robbers broke into most of the Egyptian pharaohs' tombs. They stole the treasures. Untold thousands of valuable pieces were lost. However, nobody touched the rich Tut tomb, until Howard Carter was able to find it on November 5, 1922.

The Discovery

10   Carter stumbled upon Tut's tomb while checking other ruins. He uncovered a rock stairway going down into the ground. First, workers cleared it step by step. At the bottom, they found a sealed doorway. The door had **royal** signs with Tut's name. Carter made a small hole at the top of the door. He then used a flashlight to look inside. Behind the door was a passage filled with rocks. Carter was sure he had found a major tomb.

11   Three weeks later, Carter and his crew entered the tomb. They opened the first door and started clearing the rocks. By the next day, they got to a second door. This was sealed like the first door. Again, Carter dug a hole to look inside. "Can you see anything?" someone asked. "Yes, wonderful things," Carter answered.

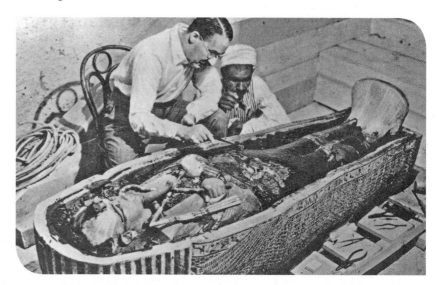

12   It was wonderful! The walls were covered with paintings about the king's life. There were beautiful couches and carved chairs. There were flowers and vases and a gold chariot. There were giant statues of gods. And between the statues was another doorway. This led to the burial **chamber**.

13   Inside the chamber was the **sarcophagus**. This was the human-shaped coffin that held Tut's **mummy**. Carter opened the top. Inside was another sarcophagus. Inside that one was a third. This final one was made of solid gold! Here was the final resting place of King Tut.

Comprehension Check

1. What details told Carter he had found an important tomb?

   a. The passage was filled with rocks.

   b. The tomb had more than one door.

   c. Ancient writings said Tut's tomb was important.

   d. The tomb's doors were sealed and had royal signs.

2. What was the room outside the burial chamber filled with?

   a. mummies

   b. rocks and dirt

   c. traps for robbers

   d. valuable treasures

3. Working with a partner, read the text to find details about what happened to most Egyptian kings' tombs. How do these details help explain the importance of Tut's tomb?

Robbers had broke into most of the tombs and stolen treasures, Tut tomb had all of of his treasures, which it was unumal.

Independent Practice

The Amazing Tomb of Tut *continued*

RI.3.2

WORDS TO KNOW
log book
original
preserved

CITE EVIDENCE

A The author describes the care the workers took with Tut's treasures. In paragraphs 15 and 16, underline details that show this.

B In the article's final section, the author restates the main idea. Circle the two sentences in paragraph 18 that do this. How did Carter's find help other scientists?

Why Did It Take So Long?

14   It took three years for Carter to go from finding the stairway to seeing Tut's mummy. It took another five years for the whole tomb to be studied. Why did it take so long?

15   All of the work was done by hand. Outside the tomb, digging was done with shovels and rakes. Workers had to pick up rocks and carry them away. Inside the tomb, special care had to be taken so that objects were not broken. Small hand brooms and rags were used to clean objects. Because of their age, many objects had to be **preserved** in place. If not, they could crumble to dust.

16   Special machines had to be built inside the tomb. These machines helped remove the golden coffin from the outer coffins. New ways of working had to be figured out so nothing was destroyed. Each piece in the tomb had to be photographed and described in a **log book**. Then the pieces were wrapped carefully and shipped to a museum.

Why Was It So Important?

17   Before Tut's, no Egyptian tombs had been found in their **original** condition. Scientists knew about ancient Egypt from writings and paintings, but they had found very few actual objects from that period.

18   The items found with Tut were beautiful and valuable. More importantly, they taught scientists much about ancient Egyptian life. The statues and artwork told about the religion. The jewelry and crafts told about the work Egyptians did. The seeds and grains told about the foods they grew and ate. The woods and metals told about other peoples the Egyptians traded with.

19   Tut's mummy itself revealed details about Egyptian royalty.
Eighty years later, scientists used modern tests on the mummy.
They learned about Tut's parents and sisters. They learned about
his health and possible reasons for his death. And they confirmed
the existence of a royal family that had been erased from
Egyptian memory.

Comprehension Check   (MORE ONLINE) **sadlierconnect.com**

1. What is the most important thing that researchers got from the
items in Tut's tomb?

   a. the value of gold in ancient Egypt

   b. information about ancient Egyptian life

   c. the honor of being the first to see them

   d. details about Tut's illness and treatment

2. What is the purpose of each section of the text?

   a. to explain the death of King Tut

   b. to tell the story of Howard Carter

   c. to support the main idea about Tut's tomb

   d. to tell what happened during King Tut's rule

3. What is the main idea of the section "Why Did It Take So Long?"
List the facts that the article uses to support the main idea.

   _It took so long_____

   _____

   _____

   _____

   _____

Guided Instruction

RI.3.3

WORDS TO KNOW

civilization
dominated
expedition
university

Look for **language** that helps you **recognize the sequence of historical events.**

CITE EVIDENCE

A Authors use dates and other **time-related words** to let the reader know the **order of events**. Circle the date in paragraph 1. In the same paragraph, underline text describing events that happened before this date.

B Draw a box around other words in both paragraphs that indicate the time of events. Why are these words so important to the reader?

Finding Machu Picchu

(Genre: Science Magazine Article)

1   It was the morning of July 24, 1911. Hiram Bingham found himself crossing a bridge on his hands and knees. He crawled over slippery logs joined with vines. The Urubamba River roared below. Bingham went slowly. His guide waited on the other side. Melchor Arteaga had crossed the bridge in bare feet, carefully. It was not the first time Bingham's **expedition** had faced danger. The mountains were steep. The jungle was full of snakes. The river was hard to cross. A week earlier, one member of the expedition had drowned in the rapids.

2   Arteaga was a local farmer. He had joined the expedition only days earlier, when the explorers camped near his home. Back at camp, Arteaga learned they were searching for ancient ruins. The farmer told Bingham there were some nearby. He said they were up the mountain, Machu Picchu. Now Arteaga led the way. They crossed the bridge and struggled through dense jungle. It was terribly hot. Arteaga brought them to the bottom of a steep slope. They climbed hard for over an hour.

RI.3.3

A Daring Professor

3   This was not Bingham's first time in Peru. He taught South American history at Yale **University**, but he had a taste for adventure. He had traveled throughout South America. He had written a book about his journeys. Now he was leading his third expedition on the continent. He had carefully planned every detail. The group aimed to explore Peru from the Urubamba River to the Pacific Ocean. They made detailed maps along the way. They collected insects, plants, and fossils. They explored ruins left behind by the Inca **civilization**.

4   The Inca had **dominated** the area centuries earlier. The remains of their buildings were found throughout Peru. In some places, roads they created were still in use. Bingham was fascinated with the Inca culture. He longed to discover a lost Incan city.

CITE EVIDENCE

C Authors often include text that helps connect the reader to a person's past. In paragraph 3, draw a box around text that tells about Bingham's life before the 1911 expedition.

D Language showing cause and effect can help the reader understand a sequence of events. Underline the effects of Bingham's third expedition to South America. What caused him to travel all over South America to begin with?

Comprehension Check

List the sequence of events in paragraph 2 (involving Melchor Arteaga) that led to the dramatic scene described in paragraph 1.

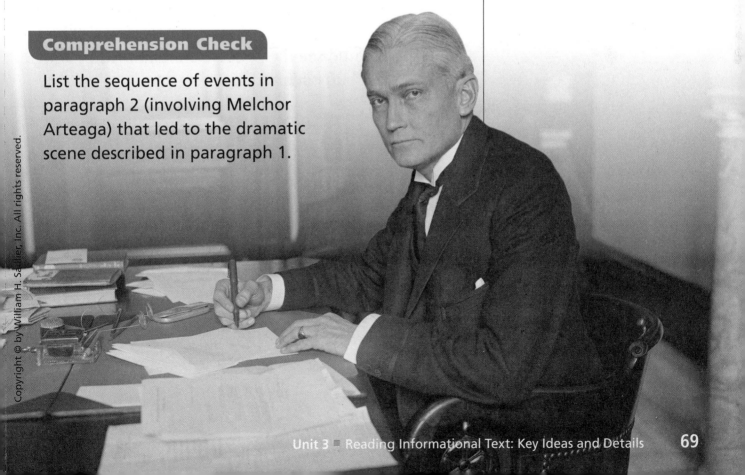

DESCRIBING RELATIONSHIPS BETWEEN IDEAS

Guided Practice

RI.3.3

WORDS TO KNOW
constructed
demonstration
labor
precise

CITE EVIDENCE

A Underline the cause that led to the following effect: "So, a young boy showed Bingham the way instead."

B Circle the words in paragraph 6 that hint at why the houses are "covered with moss." Who built these houses?

Finding Machu Picchu *continued*

A Child Leads the Way

5   The explorers reached the end of their long climb. There was a grass hut ahead. Native farmers greeted them. Bingham and his men rested in the shade. They enjoyed the view of the canyon. There were several terraces, flat steps of stone and earth. Bingham saw that the locals used the terraces for farming, just as the Inca had centuries before.

6   Local men told Bingham about ruins nearby. Bingham had heard tall tales before. He did not expect to find much. Arteaga did not seem eager to leave the shade of the huts. So, a young boy showed Bingham the way instead. The child led the explorer around a mountain ridge. As they walked, Bingham noticed the quality of stonework was improving. He crossed magnificently **constructed** terraces. He entered a forest. Suddenly, he found himself in a maze of ancient houses. The houses were made of granite, the same kind of rock as the mountain. They were covered with moss and vegetation. Still, Bingham could see the **precise** craftsmanship with which they had been built so long ago.

7   Bingham's young guide led him to a cave. The cave was lined with hand-carved stone. Above the cave there was a beautiful, rounded building. Nearby was a stone stairway. Climbing the stairs, Bingham found magnificent ruins. The walls of these ancient buildings were made of perfect, white, ten-foot-tall stone blocks. The site was a remarkable **demonstration** of the Inca's skill, **labor**, and art.

Comprehension Check

1. Who or what contributed most to Bingham's discovery of the ruins?

  a. Melchor Arteaga

  b. careful planning

  c. the young boy

  d. scientific instruments

2. Based on the text, it is most certain that

  a. the local farmers lived in stone houses built centuries earlier

  b. the local farmers knew of the ruins before Bingham did

  c. the Inca builders used metal tools after trading with explorers

  d. the Pacific Ocean climate preserved the Aztec stone work

3. The stone terraces were used for farming by both the Inca and the local people in 1911. Did the local people in Bingham's day build their own terraces? Cite evidence.

No the local people did not build there own tereses. They were there from the Anca

Independent Practice

Finding Machu Picchu *continued*

RI.3.3

WORDS TO KNOW

excavate

irrigation

theory

CITE EVIDENCE

A In paragraphs 8 and 9, underline the phrases that point to the passage of time.

B Circle information in paragraphs 10 and 11 that helps you figure out how long the Inca lived in Machu Picchu. What helped end the Inca civilization?

Palace of the Earth Shaker

8   Much has been learned about the Inca civilization at Machu Picchu since Bingham's day. People lived there and farmed. An **irrigation** system carried water through the area. About 200 buildings are set on terraces surrounding a central square. The Inca used the buildings as temples, warehouses, or homes. Their walls were designed to stand up to powerful earthquakes.

9   There is disagreement about why the Inca built Machu Picchu. Scholars have suggested several **theories**. Hiram Bingham thought that the site was the birthplace of Inca civilization. More recently, others have claimed that Machu Picchu was a religious site. A popular theory from 2008 says that Machu Picchu was a royal summer palace for the great Pachacuti.

10   Machu Picchu was built around A.D. 1450. The Inca Empire was near the height of its power. Pachacuti was its ruler. His name, which means "earth shaker," was well deserved. Through warfare, Pachacuti turned his small chiefdom into a mighty empire.

11   The Incas deserted the site about 100 years after building it. At the time, they were fighting a losing battle against Spanish soldiers. There is no evidence that the Spaniards ever discovered Machu Picchu. The site was mostly forgotten over the next few centuries. Only the local people knew of it until Bingham's arrival.

Finding Machu Picchu

12   After Bingham's discovery, other travelers claimed to have discovered the ruins before him. There is some evidence that Bingham was not the first foreigner to find the site. But he was the first to **excavate** the ruins. He photographed Machu Picchu and wrote about it in detail. It was Bingham who brought these wondrous ruins to the attention of the whole world.

Comprehension Check

MORE ONLINE   **sadlierconnect.com**

1. According to the text, until Bingham found Machu Picchu

    a. he had never seen Incan ruins

    b. he thought it was only a legend

    c. the site was completely hidden underground

    d. the site was known to only a few local people

2. What was an effect of Bingham's having found Machu Picchu?

    a. Archaeologists no longer study Machu Picchu.

    b. Scholars learned how the Inca Empire died.

    c. Machu Picchu was brought to the attention of the whole world.

    d. There is agreement about why Machu Picchu was built.

3. What caused the emperor of the Inca who built Machu Picchu to be known as "earth shaker"? Use text from the article in your answer.

    He tured his chimten into

Howard Carter's Last Chance

(Genre: Biography)

1   Howard Carter was born in London on May 9, 1874. He was a sickly child. His parents sent him to live with his aunts in the countryside. They hoped it would improve his health, but he remained too weak for sports and exercise at school. The young Carter displayed great artistic ability, however. His father, Samuel Carter, was a successful illustrator and painter. He helped Howard learn these crafts.

2   Howard's early training paid off. Through his father's influence, he was hired by an archaeologist to draw sketches. In 1891, at age 17, Carter traveled to Egypt to join in the excavation of ancient tombs. He showed great enthusiasm for his work. His original approach to depicting tomb decorations was greatly admired. With the success of his first assignment, Carter easily found more work in Egypt. He spent the next eight years at archaeological sites around the country. He worked with some of the best archaeologists of the day. He learned everything he could.

Howard Carter

RI.3.1, RI.3.2, RI.3.3, RI.3.10

3   Carter had come to Egypt as a gifted young artist. Through years of hard work, he had gained new skills. He was a good planner and manager. He was a careful excavator. He became an experienced engineer. In 1899, he was appointed chief inspector of the Egyptian Antiquities Service. As part of this job, Carter protected ancient ruins from decay. He protected ancient artifacts from tomb robbers. He approved plans for new digs. And he led many excavations himself. Carter left this job in 1905. But it was not long before his work in Egypt would continue.

Lord Carnarvon

4   His next opportunity arrived when he met George Herbert, the 5th Earl of Carnarvon. Lord Carnarvon was an English aristocrat. He was born to a very rich family. He went to the best schools in England. In an age when most people still rode horse-drawn carriages, he drove automobiles. In 1901, he was injured in a driving accident. Due to his injuries, he suffered in cold weather. To escape the cold, Lord Carnarvon began spending his winters in Egypt in 1903. In Egypt, he became interested in archaeology. He used his own money to fund expeditions. He searched the deserts for lost tombs.

5   Carnarvon's first attempts did not work out. So in 1907, he hired Howard Carter. Carter introduced Lord Carnarvon to modern techniques of excavation. He made sure that every detail of his work was recorded. Sure enough, with Carter in the lead, Carnarvon's team had some success. But all their discoveries would pale in comparison to the great find that lay ahead of them.

6   In 1914, Carnarvon received approval for a new dig. He hoped to find a lost tomb in the Valley of the Kings. He hired Howard Carter to lead the job. Archaeologists had assumed there were no more tombs to be found in the Valley of the Kings. Carter aimed to prove them wrong. He organized a team and set to work. Years passed without a major discovery. Carter's workers moved 200,000 tons of rock, sand, and earth. They achieved next to nothing. It began to seem that Carter had been mistaken. Lord Carnarvon began to lose hope. He gave Carter one last chance.

7   On November 1, 1922, Carter led his team on one last dig. At first things went no better than before. But Carter's bad luck changed on the morning of November 4. A young Egyptian boy, hired to bring water to the workers, was using a stick to dig in the ground. He was making a hole to hold a water jar. Instead, he found a stone step! Carter's crew started digging in this area immediately. They found stairs leading down to a sealed door. Could this be the entrance to Tutankhamun's tomb?

8   Carter ordered the workers to refill the hole and guard it. He made preparations to return to the site. Carnarvon was out of the country. Carter sent word to him about the find. Weeks later, Carnarvon arrived in Egypt. At last, work at the site resumed. This time, the workers cleared the stairs completely. At the bottom of the door, Carter found the seal of Tutankhamun.

9   The door was opened. Carter and Carnarvon found themselves in a dark passage full of rubble. The workers cleared the passage. They found another sealed door with the mark of Tutankhamun. Carter's hands shook as he made a small opening in the door. He saw only darkness beyond. Carter held a candle through the opening. He looked inside. The candle flickered as hot air rushed out of the chamber. Carter's eyes soon adjusted to the light. He could see the contents of the room. "Strange animals, statues, and gold," Carter would later write. "Everywhere the glint of gold."

10   Carter was in awe. He couldn't speak. Lord Carnarvon, standing beside him, couldn't stand the suspense. "Can you see anything?" he asked. "Yes," replied Carter, "wonderful things."

11   It took eight years before all those wonderful things had been removed from Tutankhamun's tomb. The tomb was remarkably complete. It was perhaps the greatest find in the history of Egyptian archaeology. The name of the man who found it will be remembered forever beside the name of Tutankhamun.

Comprehension Check

1. Based on information in the text, what was Howard Carter's success as an archaeologist mainly a result of?

   a. his father's influence

   b. his relationship with Carnarvon

   c. his skill and hard work

   d. his consistent good luck

2. What trait described in the text helped Carter most at the beginning of his career?

   a. his ability to organize and plan

   b. his knowledge of archaeological techniques

   c. his love of Egyptian history

   d. his artistic ability

3. Paragraph 10 states that "Carter was in awe" when he first saw the contents of the tomb. Describe further how Carter must have felt at this moment. What details in the text support the idea that this was the greatest event of Carter's life.

The greatest event of Carter's life is when he saw all those golds because he was very "wow!"

carter work hard too.

4. In paragraph 4, we learn that Carnarvon was injured in a car accident. Using evidence from the text, describe the series of events that links his accident to the discovery of the tomb of Tutankhamun.

The serie and event is heais in the city in the car and then he bumpt by axalent.

he waited cold winter by going to Engipt and then Howard coarter

RI.3.9, SL.3.1.a, SL.3.1.c, SL.3.1.d, SL.3.4

Compare and Contrast Texts

In this unit, you read about the discovery of Lyuba, King Tut's tomb, and Machu Picchu and Howard Carter's achievement. Choose two of these events and compare and contrast them using the Venn diagram below. List key details and other evidence from the texts to show similarities and differences. Be prepared to discuss your ideas with the class.

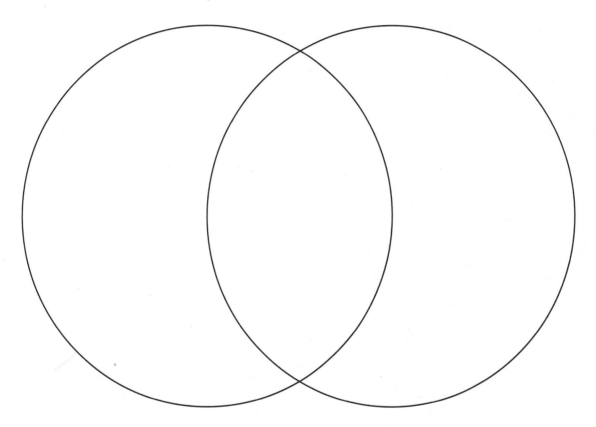

Return to the Essential Question

How do authors convey a main idea and use details to support it?

In small groups or as a class, discuss the Essential Question. Think about what you have learned about asking and answering questions, determining the main idea, and recognizing relationships in a text. Use evidence from the four unit texts to answer the question.

L.3.5.b

Real-Life Word Connections

Guided Instruction Identify **real-life word connections** with your own life. Describing your own experiences can help you practice new words, phrases, and meanings.

Lord Carnarvon "couldn't stand the suspense" while Howard Carter peered into Tutankhamun's tomb. In the example below, a student has used the same phrase to describe a personal experience.

I had to wait until after dinner to open my presents on my last birthday. Sitting at the table, I couldn't stand the suspense.

original	(*adj.*) independent and creative in thought or action
assume	(*v.*) to suppose something true without knowing the facts

Look at the chart to find definitions of two words from "Howard Carter's Last Chance." Use the definitions to complete the exercise below.

Guided Practice Use each word in the table to describe two real-life experiences.

1. _____

2. _____

3. _____

4. _____

Independent Practice Make real-life connections using the words from "Finding Machu Picchu" below. If necessary, use a dictionary to determine word meanings.

culture

_____

dominate

_____

RI.3.1, RI.3.2, RI.3.3, L.3.5.b

Read the following passage. Pay attention to the important details and the relationship between ideas to help you understand the text. Then answer the questions on pages 81 and 82.

Vikings in America

(Genre: Textbook Article)

1   Columbus was not the first person to discover the Americas. The first inhabitants of North America migrated from Asia over 16,000 years ago. There is also evidence that Vikings reached the mainland about 500 years before Columbus's journey.

2   Stories of Vikings finding North America were centuries old. Without evidence, these claims remained just legends. In 1960, however, a Norwegian explorer discovered the remains of a Viking village in northeastern Canada. The site was excavated. Many items were found. Studies of these items show that Vikings lived at the site. Workshops for metalwork, carpentry, and boat repair had things unknown to Native Americans until the arrival of Europeans. Other items associated with Viking culture were found, including a stone used to sharpen metal objects, an oil lamp, and a bronze pin. The discovery proved there was truth in the old Viking legends.

Fill in the circle of the correct answer choice.

1. Vikings came to North America

○ before anyone else

◉ 500 years before Columbus

○ only in legends

○ the same time as Columbus

2. In paragraph 2, *show* means

○ a TV program or play

○ to put on display

◉ to provide evidence

○ to teach or instruct

3. The last sentence in the article suggests that legends

   ○ can never be trusted

   ◉ sometimes contain truths

   ○ do not inform about history

   ○ are for entertainment only

4. Which technology did the Vikings use 1,000 years ago?

   ◉ metalwork

   ○ steam engines

   ○ electricity

   ○ mass production

5. Underline the word *journey* in paragraph 1, line 4. Describe a journey you have had. *befor*

   The biking Columbis for 500,

6. What is the main idea of "Vikings in America"?

   Pernaro

7. How did items that were found help prove that Vikings were in mainland North America long ago?

   The items were on known to native americans

8. Describe the series of events that is proof of the Viking legends.

   _____

   _____

9. The article mentions three "discoveries" of the Americas. List them in order.

   _____

10. Does the article provide evidence indicating whether the Vikings had sailing ships?

   _____

Introducing UNIT 4

In this unit about amazing things from our past, you will learn how to write an informative or explanatory text. When you do this kind of writing, you give information about a topic that interests you.

When you write an informative or explanatory text, you want to think carefully about the organization. You should introduce the topic in the beginning, and then group related information about the topic together. Your essay should end with a statement or paragraph that tells what the reader just learned. Linking words such as *also, another,* and *but* can help you show how ideas are related.

To be effective, an informative or explanatory text should use facts, definitions, and details to explain the ideas and develop the topic.

Progress Check *Can I?*

Before Unit 4		After Unit 4
☐	Introduce a topic.	☐
☐	Group related information together.	☐
☐	Use facts, definitions, and details to develop a topic.	☐
☐	Use linking words to connect ideas.	☐
☐	Complete my writing with a concluding statement.	☐
☐	Write using pronouns.	☐
☐	Write using pronouns and antecedents that agree.	☐
☐	Spell high-frequency words correctly.	☐
☐	Use commas in addresses.	☐

HOME◆CONNECT...

In this unit, children will learn about **writing to inform or explain a topic** to the reader. Discuss with your child different types of explanatory and informative texts, such as recipes, instruction guides, encyclopedias, informative websites, and textbooks.

Informative writing topics are developed with **facts**, **definitions**, and **details**. Ask your child to tell you about his or her writing topic, and to give details by describing something or defining a term. If your child has difficulty describing a topic, find a related image—an illustration or a photo. Encourage your child to describe the image and then incorporate some of these details into his or her writing.

Think of other topics that interest both you and your child. Together, research and write down facts and details about the topic. Have your child write an **introduction** that explains what the topic is. Then work with him or her to **link ideas** to make the writing flow. Distribute your informative text to friends or other family members.

On the Go: Encourage your child's curiosity about topics. Guide him or her to resources that can help answer questions. Model for your child how to use the Internet to search for good sources of information. Talk about different resources you use when you want to find out information or learn how to do something new.

IN THIS UNIT, YOUR CHILD WILL...

- Learn to write an informative or explanatory text that introduces a topic, groups related information, and ends with a conclusion.

- Use facts, definitions, and details to support the topic.

- Learn to use linking words, such as *also, another, more,* and *but,* to connect ideas.

- Learn specific language skills and use them in writing an explanatory or informative text:

  - Use pronouns, such as *he, we,* or *they*, to take the place of a noun.

  - Check sentences for proper pronoun agreement.

  - Spell high-frequency words correctly.

  - Use a comma between the city and state in an address.

NOTE: All of these learning goals for your child are based on the Grade 3 Common Core State Standards for English Language Arts.

WAYS TO HELP YOUR CHILD

Help your child practice using descriptive words by playing a game called "Stretch It." Choose a word such as *frog*. Take turns adding a description to the word, such as *the tiny, wet, slippery, green frog.* Discuss how writers use descriptions to explain and inform.

> **ONLINE**
> **For more Home Connect activities, continue online at** sadlierconnect.com

Text Types and Purposes: Write Informative/ Explanatory Texts

Essential Question:
How do writers develop a topic to inform or explain?

W.3.2.a

CREATING AN ORGANIZATIONAL STRUCTURE

Janine used the outline below. It is divided into three sections: introduction, explanation, and conclusion.

Title: _____

I. Introduction
   Topic: _____
   _____

II. Explanation
   Subtopic 1: _____
   Facts: _____
   _____

   Subtopic 2: _____
   Facts: _____
   _____

III. Conclusion
   _____
   _____
   _____

TITLE

Identifies the main topic for the reader

INTRODUCTION

The introduction states the topic.

Underline the pair of sentences that tell what this report is about.

Read a Student Model

Janine has been asked to write an informative/explanatory report about King Tutankhamun, a ruler in Egypt over 3,000 years ago. Janine has used an introduction to state her topic and facts to explain what she learned about King Tutankhamun. As you read her report, think about the topic for your report and how you can use facts, definitions, and details to explain it.

The Mystery of King Tut

Many people think that all of the kings of ancient Egypt were buried in the pyramids. A huge number of these rulers were actually buried in an area called the Valley of the Kings. The famous King Tutankhamun, or King Tut, was buried there. His tomb and his mummy were discovered in 1922. We have learned many things about King Tut since then. Yet, there are many things we don't know. Everyone loves a good mystery. This may be why people continue to be so interested in King Tut.

W.3.2.a–c

King Tut's MRI Results

King Tut became a ruler in Egypt when he was young. He ruled for only nine years. In 2013, an MRI was used to look at his mummy. An MRI is a special scanner that takes pictures and sends them to a computer. From the pictures, scientists learned that Tut was around 19 years old when he died.

DEVELOP THE TOPIC

Facts, definitions, and details help the reader understand the topic.

In this section, underline a fact and circle a word and its definition.

Many people wonder why King Tut died so young. One rumor said that he was hit from behind. The MRI scans of his head, however, did not show he had been hit. Another idea was that he was hurt in battle. One scan did find a broken bone above his knee. Scientists do not know when this happened, but it could have happened when the mummy was first moved.

ORGANIZATION

Related information is grouped together.

Put boxes around two sentences that tell what scientists learned about King Tut's body.

Was King Tut Sick?

Scientists thought King Tut's foot looked odd. In 2003, they took DNA from his mummy. The DNA showed that some of the bone had died. It may have made King Tut limp and use a cane. Still, the scientists do not think this killed King Tut. Scientists also took DNA from an ancient insect in the pyramid. The insect carried a disease called malaria. This disease can be deadly. However, they do not know if this caused his death.

LINKING WORDS

Linking words (such as *and*, *also*, and *but*) and phrases help connect the ideas.

Circle the linking words in the section "Was King Tut Sick?"

W.3.2.d

CONCLUSION

The conclusion wraps up the topic by telling what was learned. It also adds an interesting idea related to the topic.

Underline the concluding statement.

What caused this young ruler to die? He was not hit in the head. He did not die from a deformed foot. Did he get sick? Was it something else? The scans and tests ruled out some ideas. Yet, we still are not sure what caused King Tut to die so young. As scientists invent new tests and technology, they may find the answers to some of these questions. Until then, King Tut will be remembered as much for what we do know as for what we still wonder.

W.3.2.a–d, W.3.4, W.3.5, W.3.10

Use an outline like the one below to organize your informative/
explanatory essay on a history or science topic that interests you.
Then write a first draft of your essay on a separate sheet of paper.
Make sure to develop your topic using facts and details and group
related information together. Remember to use linking words in
your draft to connect pieces of information. Lastly, make sure your
draft ends with a conclusion that summarizes your topic. You will use
this draft to write your final essay in the Common Core Review
section on page 96.

Title: What Rosa Park Did

I. **Introduction**
   Topic: Rosa Park

II. **Explanation**
   Subtopic 1: About Rosa Park
   Facts: Rosa Park has a brother. She is very
   brave, she stood up and made a difference.

   Subtopic 2: What she did
   Facts: One day, Rosa Parks was going to
   go on the back of the bus she couldn't
   because it was to crowded.

III. **Conclusion**
   So, she went to the front of the door
   but then the bus driver got mad because
   black can not go on the front they are
   suppost to go and on the back of the bus. She
   sit the whole time but, the bus driver said
   to get out of his bus. She did not move. Then he called cops.

L.3.1.a

Pronouns

Guided Instruction A **pronoun** takes the place of a noun. Some of the most common pronouns are *I, he, she, it, we, they,* and *you.*

Statues *were found in China.* [noun]
They *were found in China.* [pronoun]

The **Emperor** *had the statues made.* [noun]
He *had the statues made.* [pronoun]

The **book** *is from the museum gift shop.* [noun]
It *is from the museum gift shop.* [pronoun]

Guided Practice Write the pronoun in each sentence.

1. We went to the museum to see the Terra Cotta Warriors. _____We_____

2. Suprisingly, she knew a lot about them. _____She_____

3. Have you heard of the statues? _____you_____

4. They are very old statues of warriors. _____they_____

5. I liked how each statue looked different. _____I_____

Independent Practice Replace the underlined words with a pronoun.

1. Mrs. Ling is our teacher. _____She_____

2. Mrs. Ling took us to see the exhibit. _____it_____

3. Our class saw pictures of the pits where the warriors were found. _____We_____

4. The guides told us how they found the warriors. _____they_____

5. Mr. Hurd showed us the tools they used. _____he_____

Pronoun-Antecedent Agreement

Guided Instruction Some pronouns have antecedents. The **antecedent** is the noun the pronoun refers to. The pronoun and antecedent must match. Both must be singular or plural.

*The **scientists** work for **their** museum.*
　　[antecedent]　　　[pronoun]

*The **scientist** works for **her** museum.*
　　[antecedent]　　　[pronoun]

Guided Practice Correct the sentences.

1. The tourists brought his camera.

   The tourists brought their camera.

   _____

2. Kayla left its camera on the bus.

   Kayla left her camera on the bus.

   _____

3. The students took pictures of her visit to the pyramid.

   The students took pictures of their vist to
   the pyramid.

4. Curt and Diego drew pictures of his favorite sites.

   Curt and Diego drew pictures of their favorite
   sites.

Independent Practice Use a pronoun and antecedent in a sentence. Underline the pronoun and its antecedent.

_____

_____

Spelling High-Frequency Words

Guided Instruction It is important to spell words correctly when you are writing. You should remember how to spell high-frequency words that you use often when you write.

High-Frequency Words		
another	especially	question
believe	friendly	ready
caught	important	thought
does	knew	usually

Guided Practice Circle the correct spelling of the word in parentheses.

1. Chichen Itza is an (importent, (important)) pyramid in Mexico.

2. Scientists ((believe), beleeve) that the Mayans built the pyramid.

3. (Anuther, (Another)) Mayan pyramid is El Castillo.

4. Pyramids were (espeshelly, (especially)) important in Mayan society.

Independent Practice Find the misspelled word and spell it correctly on the line.

1. Chichen Itza has meny steps leading to the top. _many_

2. Some peeple like to climb the stairs. _people_

3. You should place your feet carfully as you climb, so you don't fall. _cerfully_

4. Be reddy for a tough climb, but know that it is well worth it in the end. _ready_

Unit 4 ■ Text Types and Purposes: Write Informative/Explanatory Texts

Commas in Addresses

Guided Instruction A comma is used to separate words or ideas. In an address, a comma separates a city from a state.

Dinosaur National Monument
4545 E. Highway 40
Dinosaur, CO 81610

Guided Practice Add a comma to the sentences below.

1. Dinosaur National Park is near Boulder, Colorado.

2. On your way to the park, you may want to visit the craters near Twin Falls, Idaho.

3. You can also travel to Salt Lake City, Utah, which is nearby.

Independent Practice Using correct punctuation, write your address below.

Samantha Wong
18 street
New Hyde Park, New York 1140

SL.3.1.a–d, SL.3.3

Discuss the Essential Question

How do writers develop a topic to inform or explain?

Think about the Essential Question by responding to the questions below. Support your point of view with reasons and experience.

1. How does the writer of "The Mystery of King Tut" group related information, or facts, together?

   _____

   _____

2. What linking words does the writer of "The Mystery of King Tut" use to connect ideas?

   _____

   _____

Use your notes above to discuss the Essential Question in small groups or as a class. Follow agreed-upon rules for discussion. Use the organizer below to record what you heard and how you participated.

Ideas I Agree or Disagree With		Questions I Asked
Agree		
Disagree		
New Ideas I Had During Discussion		**Questions I Answered**

L.3.1.a, L.3.1.f, L.3.2.b, L.3.2.e

This letter has mistakes in spelling, punctuation, and use of pronouns. Write the paragraph correctly on the lines below.

238 Elm Street
Nashville TN 37240

Dear Dr. Frank,

I would like to ask your a few questuns. I am intrested in how you use planes to map your sites. How did your team members get his information about Peru? Do you beleeve that technology will help you find more artifacts? Thank you for the infermation.

Tomas

238 Elm Street Nashville, TN 37240

Nashville, TN 37240

Dear Dr. Frank,

I would like to ask you a few questions.
I am interested in how you use planes
to map sites. Wow did your team members
get their information about Peru?
Do you believe that technology will help
you find more artifacts

Thank you for th information

Tomas

W.3.2.a–d, W.3.4, W.3.5, W.3.10

Assignment: Write an informative/explanatory text about a history or science topic that interests you.

On the lines below, write your final copy of the informative/explanatory essay you created on page 89. Be sure to introduce the topic and end with a concluding sentence or paragraph. Make sure to use facts, definitions, and details to explain the topic. Do not forget to use linking words to connect ideas. See the Writing Handbook (pages 275–283) for ways to improve your writing as you revise.

_____

_____

_____

_____

_____

_____

_____

_____

_____

_____

_____

_____

_____

_____

_____

_____

Introducing UNIT 5

What makes friendship special? Do you take time to look for and keep good friends? In this unit, you will read about different pairs of best friends who help each other to be their best.

In the fiction selections that follow, you will look at how authors use language. You will read examples of literal language, where authors say just what they mean, and nonliteral language, where authors use words to create images or associations. You will also find examples of different text structures, including a drama and a narrative poem. As you read, you can look at how fiction can present points of view that may be different from your own.

Learning about the craft and structure of the works that follow will help you better understand the stories of friendship. Then you can talk about them with a friend!

Before Unit 5 ⬇

Progress Check *Can I?*

After Unit 5 ⬇

☐ Understand literal and nonliteral language. ☐

☐ Recognize the different parts of a drama. ☐

☐ Distinguish my point of view from those of the narrator and characters. ☐

HOME ◆ CONNECT...

Creative writers use **nonliteral** phrases to create images in a reader's mind. The **literal**, or actual, meaning of the words might be different from what the author is really trying to say. Help your child see the difference. In a children's story or poem, highlight a phrase that is not meant literally. Talk with your child about what it means. Have your child find other examples.

Good readers can talk about the parts of stories, poems, and plays. To help your child understand the **parts of a drama**, find a children's play online or in the library. Read it together, and talk about what happens in each scene. Discuss how scenes in a play are like chapters in a book.

In stories, a narrator or character often feels strongly about something. Readers learn to understand those **points of view** and distinguish them from their own. Read together a children's story or play with a strong point of view. Ask your child about the narrator or character's feelings. Discuss whether you both share these feelings.

 Conversation Starter: With your child, talk about a favorite story. Ask your child:

- *Can you name examples of figurative language or idioms in the story? What are they?*
- *If you turned the story into a play, how many scenes would there be? What would happen in each scene?*
- *How would you describe the main character's point of view? Do you agree with that point of view?*

IN THIS UNIT, YOUR CHILD WILL...

- Figure out the meanings of unfamiliar words in texts.

- Distinguish literal language from figurative words and phrases, such as idioms.

- Understand parts of a drama, including scenes, setting, character list, and stage directions.

- Understand the point of view of a narrator or character in a story and distinguish it from his or her own point of view.

- Compare and contrast four texts with the same theme: realistic fiction, drama, a narrative poem, and historical fiction.

NOTE: All of these learning goals for your child are based on the Grade 3 Common Core State Standards for English Language Arts.

WAYS TO HELP YOUR CHILD

Help your child understand how writers use language to spur readers' imaginations. Read stories and poems together, and point out lines and phrases that you particularly enjoy. Encourage your child to find examples of favorites, too. You might also listen for oral langauge that creates images on the internet, radio, or television.

ONLINE

For more Home Connect activities, continue online at sadlierconnect.com

Reading Literature: Craft and Structure

UNIT 5

Essential Question:
How do authors craft stories?

Guided Instruction

RL.3.4

WORDS TO KNOW

instructor
mature
mobility
orientation

Nonliteral language gives different meanings to **words and phrases** from those of **literal language**.

CITE EVIDENCE

A Writers may use **literal words** that say exactly what they mean. Or they may use **nonliteral, figurative words** that mean something other than what the words say. Circle the nonliteral word in paragraph 1, sentence 1. What is the literal meaning of the word? What does the word mean here?

The Best Friend Possible

(Genre: Realistic Fiction)

1   When Ms. Kehoe told me I could try to get a guide dog, I flipped! I've been blind since I was nine months old, and I have ALWAYS wanted a guide dog. Most organizations won't give a dog to anyone under 18. I'm only 11. Ms. Kehoe is my **orientation** and **mobility instructor**. That means she helps me learn to get around safely. She knew better than anyone how much I wanted a dog, and she found an organization that gives guide dogs to blind people between 11 and 18 years old.

2   My parents weren't sure it was a good idea. "Honey, you get around with your cane very well," my mother said. "Do you really think you need a dog?"

3   "Mom, a dog can signal what's around me. Yes, a cane is good, but a dog is better!"

4   "But a dog could be trouble," added my dad. "What if it starts to bite?"

5   "Don't worry! These dogs are trained for at least 18 months. They behave better than I do!" I laughed.

6   "But what about the money?" he argued. "A dog like that must <u>cost an arm and a leg</u>."

7   "Dad, you don't have to worry about money. The organization donates the dogs. The main problem will be that we'll probably have to wait a million years for a dog. Come on, let's look at how to join the program."

8   My parents had finally run out of arguments. Together, we <u>filled</u> out an application and started the long wait for a dog.

9   Every day, I asked my mother if the guide dog people had called. Every day, the answer was no. Finally, after many months, the answer was yes! They said that I could come to meet some guide dogs. I was <u>over the moon!</u> By now, my parents were excited about a guide dog, too. They knew that they could count on me. Not many 11-year-old girls could handle the responsibility of caring for a service dog, but I've always been **mature**.

CITE EVIDENCE

B Idioms are figurative language phrases that are usually used in informal writing and speech. Circle the idiom in paragraph 6. What does this idiom mean?

C Context clues can help you figure out literal meanings of unfamiliar words. Look for hints in surrounding words to help you understand a word. Circle the word *application* in paragraph 8. Then underline the surrounding words that help you figure out its meaning.

D Find and box the idiom in paragraph 9. What does this idiom mean?

Comprehension Check

Reread paragraph 9. Find the phrase "count on me" in sentence 7. What does the narrator mean?

The Best Friend Possible *continued*

RL.3.4

WORDS TO KNOW

bond
isolated
nonprofit organization

CITE EVIDENCE

A Reread paragraph 11. Underline the phrase *raring to go* in sentence 6. What does it mean?

B Reread paragraph 12. Circle the idiom that means "excited and nervous." Why did the author use this expression?

10   Since I don't remember being able to see, being blind is what I know. I go to a regular public school in the small town where I live, and I do pretty well. Still, I'm the only kid who is blind at the school. A dog might help me feel less **isolated**. Not only would it help me get around—it might even help me make friends!

11   There was just one hitch. I'd have to go to the **nonprofit organization** in Canada for a month to get to know a service dog and learn how to work with it. My father is a teacher, so he had time in the summer. Before long, our plans were set. We would travel near Montreal to meet some guide dogs. I was raring to go!

12   I did have one other worry. The guide dog people said that they couldn't promise that I would get a dog. They had only six dogs ready to work as guide dogs, and other kids were coming, too. It's really important that a guide dog forms a strong **bond** with its human. Sometimes, there just isn't the right dog for a person (or person for a dog). I was on pins and needles. What if none of the dogs liked me? I tried not to lose heart.

13   Finally, the day came when my father and I left for Montreal. My mother broke down at the airport, but I promised to stay in touch.

14   When we got there, I met some teenagers who were also hoping to get a guide dog. At age 11, I was the spring chicken in this group!

Comprehension Check

1. Circle the letter that shows a nonliteral phrase in the story.

   a. *the right dog for a person*

   b. *my father and I left for Montreal*

   c. *was the spring chicken*

   d. *ready to work as guide dogs*

2. Circle the letter that tells what the phrase *broke down* means in paragraph 13.

   a. The narrator's mother stopped walking.

   b. The narrator's mother started crying.

   c. The narrator's mother fell on the ground.

   d. The narrator's mother stopped showing emotion.

3. Work with a partner. Reread paragraph 12. Discuss the phrase *lose heart* in sentence 8. What does the phrase mean here? Why is the narrator trying not to lose heart?

It means to not give up hope.

RL.3.4

Independent Practice

The Best Friend Possible *continued*

WORDS TO KNOW

assign
evaluate
specialist
suspense

CITE EVIDENCE

A Reread the first sentence in paragraph 17. Underline the figurative word that suggests an image in the sentence.

B Reread paragraph 18. Circle an idiom that has to do with being nervous. What feelings do these words give you about the narrator?

15   The **specialists** said we would each work with several dogs. That way, they could **evaluate** which dog worked best with each of us. By the end of the week, if all went well, we would be **assigned** a dog.

16   "Did you like your first day?" Dad asked me that night. I had to admit it was really nice to be around other people who knew what it was like to be blind.

17   The next few days were a haze. It was really tiring to spend all day learning how to work with the dogs, but I loved meeting the different animals. Most of them were a mix of Bernese Mountain Dogs and Labradors. They're known as Labernese, and they're big and smart and lovable. All of them had been trained how to follow commands since they were puppies. We traveled on paths in a park. I tried to get used to the feeling of walking with a guide dog. When we were done working, we could play with the dogs.

18   On the fifth day, I worked with a really friendly dog named Metro. I liked all the dogs but Metro seemed special. He responded to my commands before I finished saying them. I could only hope the specialists thought we clicked as well as I did. And what if they didn't think I'd make a good partner for any of the dogs? The **suspense** was killing me.

19   Finally, Saturday came—the day I'd find out which dog (if any) would be my partner. I really enjoyed working with all of the dogs, but Metro had my HEART.

20   The specialist called, "Maxine, you'll partner up with Monk. Jorge, you'll work with Muppet. Nashaya, you'll work with Minty. Lucy, Mosh will be your guide dog. Carl, you'll work with Millie." I heard the dogs come to the teenagers. Why wasn't my name being called?

21   Finally, the specialist said, "Oh, I almost forgot! Amanda, you work with Metro." My heart leaped! Before I knew it, Metro was at my feet. We had a lot to learn, but we would learn it together.

Comprehension Check

(MORE ONLINE) **sadlierconnect.com**

1. Circle the letter that tells what the word *clicked* means in paragraph 18, sentence 4.

   a. made a snapping sound

   b. pressed, like a button

   c. got along well

   d. made things fall apart

2. Circle the letter that tells what the phrase *had my heart* means in paragraph 19.

   a. had my love

   b. worried me

   c. tugged at me

   d. made me sad

3. Why do you think an author might use idioms and other nonliteral language?

The author wants to make it
cool.
_____

Guided Instruction

RL.3.5

WORDS TO KNOW

bragging
invisible
proportion

Refer to and explain the importance of the parts of a **drama**, including **setting**, **stage direction**, and **scene**.

CITE EVIDENCE

A A **drama** has many parts. A list of **characters** tells who is in the play. Circle the characters in this play.

B The **setting** tells where and when the play takes place. Underline the setting for Scene 1. Why is the setting important?

Singing Your Blues Away

(Genre: Drama)

CHARACTERS

Nathan, a 10-year-old boy who plays the guitar
Fremont, Nathan's friend, also a 10-year-old boy
Kevin, Fremont's brother, 12, a soccer player
Mr. and Mrs. Jones, Kevin and Fremont's parents
Mrs. Ordway, Nathan's mother

Scene 1

A playground at an elementary school during recess in late autumn.

1 **NATHAN:** Hey, Fremont, what's got you down?

FREMONT: Same old story. My brother's got a soccer tournament this weekend and that's all anyone in the family can talk about. I hear my parents on the phone talking to *their* parents, **bragging** about Kevin all the time.

NATHAN: Well, he is pretty good, you know.

FREMONT: Believe me, I KNOW. Look, I'm proud of him, too, but I'm beginning to feel **invisible**.

5 **NATHAN:** Try not to blow it out of **proportion**. At least they're not worrying about you.

FREMONT: What do you mean?

NATHAN: My parents get all worried that I spend too much time alone—just because I like to spend my time playing guitar. What's so wrong with that?

FREMONT: Nothing, I'm pretty sure. Hey, what kind of music do you play?

NATHAN: Well, I'm just learning, really, but I could play you a few songs I know sometime. Hey, you want to come over after school?

10 **FREMONT:** Sure. But don't you have to check with your parents?

NATHAN: They won't mind. They'll be happy I'm bringing a friend home.

FREMONT: All right. There are two things going for this plan. One: I get to hear you play your songs. Two: I won't have to hear about Kevin the Great every minute. (*laughs*)

(*Bell rings. Kids head to classroom doors.*)

NATHAN: Cool. See you after school.

Guided Instruction

CITE EVIDENCE

C **Stage directions** tell what the characters in a drama are supposed to do. Underline the two stage directions on this page.

D **Scenes** are parts of a play. Just like with chapters in a book, each new scene in a play builds on the one before. Put a star next to the end of the scene. Since this is Scene 1, you know that more scenes will follow. Why might a play have more than one scene?

Comprehension Check

How does the setting help you better understand what's happening in the drama?

UNDERSTANDING PARTS OF A DRAMA

Guided Practice

RL.3.5

WORDS TO KNOW

spotlight
tradition

CITE EVIDENCE

A Put a star next to the last line of dialogue in Scene 2 and the first line of dialogue in Scene 3.

B Circle the setting for Scene 3. How is this setting different from the setting for Scene 2?

Singing Your Blues Away *continued*

Scene 2

The kitchen in Nathan's house in the afternoon.

(*Nathan is strumming on his guitar. Fremont starts to sing some made-up words.*)

NATHAN: (*smiling*) Hey, nice voice!

15 **FREMONT:** (*surprised*) Thanks, Nathan. You sound really good on the guitar.

(*Mrs. Ordway pokes her head in.*)

MRS. ORDWAY: You guys should take that act on the road! (*laughing*) Really, you sound great. (*She leaves.*)

FREMONT: Hey, Nathan, I think I've got an idea. You know how your parents are worried you spend too much time alone?

NATHAN: Yeah.

FREMONT: And you know how my brother gets all the attention because of his soccer?

20 **NATHAN:** Uh-huh. What's your idea?

FREMONT: This Saturday, there's a soccer family picnic. A bunch of kids from school will be there.

NATHAN: But why would you want to go to that? You don't even like soccer.

FREMONT: True, but there's a **tradition** of people giving speeches and stuff. I'm thinking we could surprise everyone and play a song.

NATHAN: Really? I like it. But what song can we play?

25 **FREMONT:** I say we write one ourselves.

NATHAN: I say okay!

Scene 3

A park in late fall. Families with children in soccer uniforms are gathered.

MRS. JONES: Kevin, we're so proud of you!

MR. JONES: You really helped your team out there, son.

KEVIN: Thanks, Dad.

(*Behind them, Fremont nods to Nathan.*)

30 **NATHAN:** (*picking up his guitar*) Are you ready to grab some **spotlight**?

FREMONT: (*smiling*) It's now or never.

Comprehension Check

1. What do Nathan and Fremont do in Scene 2?

   a. They play a song at a soccer picnic.

   b. They meet at the playground and discuss their problems.

   c. They go to a picnic and hear Mr. and Mrs. Jones praising Kevin.

   d. They play and sing and decide to play a song at a picnic.

2. What new characters are introduced in Scene 3?

   a. Mr. Jones, Mrs. Jones, Kevin

   b. Mrs. Ordway, Nathan, Fremont

   c. Mr. Jones, Mrs. Jones, Fremont

   d. Kevin, Mrs. Ordway, Mrs. Jones

3. How does Scene 2 build on what happened in Scene 1?

Scene 1 they dicass their problem and Scene 2 they have a soulusion.

UNDERSTANDING PARTS OF A DRAMA

Independent Practice

RL.3.5

WORDS TO KNOW
applaud
react
strum

CITE EVIDENCE

A Put a star next to the information that helps you understand where the two boys are when they perform in the scene.

B Circle the last line of dialogue in the scene. Why did the writer break the play into three scenes?

Singing Your Blues Away *continued*

Scene 3 *continued*

(*The two boys walk to the center of a stage, where a microphone stands.*)

FREMONT: (*speaking into microphone*) Hi, everybody. I'm Kevin's brother Fremont, and this is my buddy, Nathan.

NATHAN: Today, we want to sing a song to celebrate the soccer season. Ready?

(*People are unsure how to* **react***. A few people start to clap, then stop.*)

NATHAN AND FREMONT: (*singing*)
Everybody's good at something.
Everybody has a skill.
You all love to play soccer,
And you never have your fill.
(*Chorus*) So play that soccer, heroes.
Just play it while you can.
Your families love to watch you,
And we are all your fans.

35 **FREMONT:** So while Nathan **strums** his guitar,
And while I sing out the song,
We will celebrate your season,
And you can sing along—(*shouts*) Everybody now!
(*Chorus*) So play that soccer, heroes.
Just play it while you can.
Your families love to watch you,
And we are all your fans.

(*Crowd* **applauds** *wildly, as Nathan and Fremont bow and walk back to Fremont's family.*)

KEVIN: (*slapping Fremont on the back*) You're okay, little bro.

FREMONT: (*smiling*) Thanks, Kevin. (*looks at Nathan*) Thanks, Nathan.

NATHAN: Thank *you* for getting me out of the house!

FREMONT: (*laughing as he nudges Nathan*) Thanks to our song for helping us both out!

(*Nathan strums some exit music as curtain closes.*)

Comprehension Check

MORE ONLINE sadlierconnect.com

1. What happens in Scene 3 that the boys prepared for in Scene 2?

   a. Nathan and Fremont talk to Mrs. Ordway.

   b. Nathan and Fremont sing at the picnic.

   c. Nathan and Fremont write a song for the picnic.

   d. Nathan and Fremont meet at school.

2. How is Fremont different at the end of Scene 3 from how he was in the first scene?

   a. He is sad.

   b. He is scared.

   c. He is happy.

   d. He is jealous.

3. Why did the writer continue Scene 3 on page 110, rather than begin a new scene?

   Because the setting stays the same
   because it would not make sense.

DISTINGUISHING POINTS OF VIEW

Guided Instruction

RL.3.6

WORDS TO KNOW

embarrassed

sulked

treasure

A reader may have a different **point of view** from that of a text's narrator or characters.

CITE EVIDENCE

A Pronouns can help you figure out to whom a **point of view** belongs. Circle all the pronouns in stanza 2.

B How many characters are in this poem? Put a star by each character name.

Forever Friends
(Genre: Narrative Poem)

1 In any life, people come and they go;
   I know; I've had many a friend.
   But while some friendships have lasted,
   Others have come to an end.
   I've heard about friendships, and
   I've been glad that I had
   Friends so good, so great,
   Why, they've always been rad.

2 For friendship, dear friendship,
   Is more precious than gold.
   It's more valued than money:
   Onto it you must hold.
   Though you can't spend a friend,
   What you earn you should **treasure**.
   You can earn it and save it,
   And that's a great pleasure.

3 Think of what happened
   To young Jack and Jane.
   They were fast friends soon as Jack
   Came into town on a plane.
   When he showed up,
   The new kid in town,
   Three older boys teased him
   And put poor Jack down.

4 Though she'd only just met him,
   Jane thought Jack no fool.
   She told the three bullies,
   "Knock it off, guys, he's cool."

Embarrassed by her scolding,
The boys slunk away,
And Jack and Jane have
Been friends to this day.

5 From that day on,
Jack and Jane were not parted.
They did all together,
And couldn't wait to get started.
When Jack didn't feel well,
Jane for him would care.
When Jane forgot lunch money,
Jack would always share.

6 When Jane's dog got sick,
Jack stayed by her side,
Came along to the vet,
And filled her with pride.
When Jack got braces, he **sulked**;
His teeth were too sore.
But Jane made jokes,
And he laughed once more.

7 Sometimes other kids got jealous
Of what Jack and Jane had.
They tried separating the friends,
Or making them mad.
But Jack and Jane
Could see through it all.
They vowed never to part,
Since they were having a ball.

CITE EVIDENCE

C Use of comparisons can show a character's or narrator's point of view. Underline where the writer compares things to friendship in stanza 2. Do you agree or disagree with these ideas?

D Third-person pronouns (such as *he* and *her*) can indicate point of view. Box each third-person pronoun in stanza 6. What do they tell you about how these characters view friendship?

Comprehension Check

How do the descriptive words in this passage help you understand what the narrator, Jack, and Jane each think about friendship?

Jack and Jane each think about friendship by stayin together.

Guided Practice

Forever Friends *continued*

RL.3.6

WORDS TO KNOW

interfere
prospect
separated

CITE EVIDENCE

A Find and circle the two stanzas that are from the narrator's point of view.

B Underline the words in stanza 11 that show Jane's feelings about her friendship with Jack. How would you feel about moving away from a best friend?

8   Jack and Jane never imagined
    They'd be **separated**.
    They were always together,
    As though it were fated.
    Each day after school,
    They'd race to the park,
    And play knights and aliens
    Until it got dark.

9   Now let me just say,
    If I'd friends like these,
    I'd be beside myself;
    Life would be full of ease.
    It's not easy to find
    A good friend like this:
    Someone who stays by your side.
    Someone you'd miss.

10 But sometimes such friendships
    Aren't up to just us.
    Life **interferes**,
    And creates a fuss.
    This was the case
    For Jack and for Jane,
    As later that year,
    Bad news fell like rain.

11 While Jack was relaxing,
    It was Jane's turn to worry.
    Her mom had a new job;
    They had to move in a hurry.
    Jane wasn't ready; she loved
    School and Jack too.
    And the **prospect** of leaving
    Made her feel really blue.

12   Thoughts of telling Jack
Filled her with dread.
Sure enough, when she told him,
He was so mad he saw red.
"It's not fair," he cried,
"You're my best friend!
"I don't want to lose you.
"Will this be the end?"

Comprehension Check

1. According to stanzas 9 and 10, what does the narrator think about Jack and Jane's friendship?

   a. The narrator wishes he or she had a friendship like this.

   b. The narrator explains that he's actually Jack in disguise.

   c. The narrator says that she had a friend like this once.

   d. The narrator states that all good friendships must end.

2. What problem do Jack and Jane face at this point in their friendship?

   a. Jack is moving away and wants Jane to come with him.

   b. Jane is transferring schools, but will stay in the same town.

   c. Jack has decided that he needs other friends besides Jane.

   d. Jane is moving away, but they still want to be friends.

3. What is the narrator's point of view about friendship? Point out descriptive words used by the narrator to support your answer. Is your point of view the same as the narrator's? Explain.

   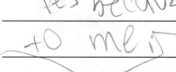 Yes because friend ship is important to me.

Independent Practice

Forever Friends *continued*

RL.3.6

WORDS TO KNOW

anew
imperiously

CITE EVIDENCE

A Underline each word that describes Jack's feelings in stanzas 13 and 14.

B Put a star by each of the ideas Jack and Jane have to keep their friendship going in stanza 15. What will they try to do?

13 "Me neither," said Jane.
"But what will we do?
"I'm moving next week;
"How will we stay true?"
"We need a solution,"
Jack said oh so seriously.
"You mustn't forget me," Jane
Ordered **imperiously**.

14 "What, me? Forget you?"
Jack said, downhearted.
"But please promise to help me
Keep up what we've started."
"It's a deal," said Jane.
"Shake on it, will you?"
They shook hands, and with that
Started planning **anew**.

15 Then, "Oh, no," Jane added.
"I'll be all alone,
"With no friends in sight—"
Jack interrupted, "Just phone.
"Call me whenever,
"And I'll call you too."
"Of course, we can e-mail,"
Jane added. "Well, phew!"

RL.3.6

16 "We'll always be friends,"
Jack promised, "I swear.
"And one of these days,
"You'll come back. That's just fair."
Jane smiled. "Until then,
"We'll text, talk, and phone.
"You'll tell me what's new,
"And I won't feel alone."

Comprehension Check

MORE ONLINE   sadlierconnect.com

1. Who is most worried about being alone?

   a. Jane

   b. Jack

   c. the narrator

   d. Jane and Jack

2. Which term below best describes Jane's point of view in stanza 13 about the future of their friendship?

   a. nervous

   b. relaxed

   c. happy

   d. jealous

3. In the end, what viewpoint do Jack and Jane share about their future as friends? Do you have the same viewpoint about their future? Use the poem and your own experiences to explain.

_____

_____

_____

We Must See the Queen!

(Genre: Historical Fiction)

Chapter 1

June 28, 1838

1   It was a beautiful day. Mariah was squirming with excitement as soon as she woke up. It was June 28, a day she and her best friend, Laura, who was a few years older, had been looking forward to for months. Today, Victoria would be crowned Queen of Britain.

2   There was going to be a huge parade in the Queen's honor. Mariah and Laura really wanted to go. Things like this didn't happen every day. It was a once-in-a-lifetime experience.

3   Mariah and Laura had spent weeks begging their parents for permission to watch the parade. "Opportunities like this don't grow on trees, Mama!" Mariah said at one point. "Please, can we go?"

4   Her mother had rolled her eyes, having already said she wasn't sure it was a good idea. "Hope springs eternal, eh? Young lady, why do you want to go so badly?"

5   Mariah had clasped her hands together, and her eyes had gleamed with excitement, like two blue stars. "Because it may be my only chance ever to see the Queen! And it's the best day to see her, because it's the day she becomes Queen!"

6   Eventually, Mariah had won, and so had Laura. The two of them were getting to go to the parade.

RL.3.4, RL.3.5, RL.3.6, RL.3.10

Chapter 2

7   After breakfast that morning, Mariah hurried over to Laura's house. She didn't have far to go to pick up her best friend. Laura, who was like her big sister, lived just next door. As she rushed past the beautiful old house, Mariah only got more excited. Today, she'd get to see the most famous woman in the world.

8   When she got to Laura's house, Mariah didn't even have to ring the bell. Laura was waiting for her in the courtyard. The two girls hugged, and then Laura tugged on her best friend's sleeve. "We'd better go, Mariah. I don't want to miss anything!"

9   The girls set off on their way to Constitution Hill. Once they got there, they'd be perfectly set up to watch the whole parade, especially the arrival of Queen Victoria.

10   After a few blocks, though, they had a problem. The roads were full of people who were all dressed up for the coronation. It seemed as if people were getting more excited with every passing minute. They were shooting around like hot sparks from a fireplace. They were talking loudly, pushing, and shoving as they tried to get closer to the parade route.

11   Mariah's head started aching with worry. She knew she could count on Laura to figure something out, though. "What should we do, Laura? Do you think we have any chance of getting there in time?"

12   Laura frowned. She wrinkled her forehead like she always did when she concentrated. This made her face as full of creases as an old map. "Hold on, Mariah, let me think." She paused for a few seconds. "What if we cut through the butcher shop? You'll have to be careful not to get your dress dirty," she added, since Mariah was pretty clumsy. "And of course it'll have to be our secret."

13   "Sure!" said Mariah happily. What were best friends for, after all, if they couldn't share secrets? She and Laura were keeping several secrets already. One was their dislike of the Brickstones' nanny. Another was Laura's wish to someday become an actress. Keeping their shortcut a secret would be a piece of cake. "All right, let's go! Hold on to your hat, Laura," Mariah called over her shoulder as they began to run.

14   The two girls raced across the street to the butcher's. There, they slid through the door and around the greasy counter. The store was much emptier than usual. All the customers were probably on their way to the parade, too.

15   Laura and Mariah ran past the cashier on duty. He looked at them with surprise and maybe a bit of envy. *He's probably jealous he can't go to the parade with us*, Mariah thought. She grinned at her best friend. The two girls hurried to the back of the shop and scampered through the back door.

16   Mariah and Laura stepped into a much less busy street. Now they were one step closer to Constitution Hill. There were only a few blocks to go. They should arrive at the route with plenty of time to see the whole parade.

17   The girls hurried down the street and made a right at the corner by the hat seller's. Just another block and they'd be at the route. Too excited to wait any longer, Mariah broke into a sprint. "Wait for me!" Laura called out.

18   Mariah looked back over her shoulder but didn't stop. "Come on, you slowpoke! What are you waiting for?"

19   Mariah then bumped straight into a group of people. "Oh, no!" she sighed as Laura caught up and rounded the corner. Laura yelled back, "It's almost as crowded here as it was before!"

20   Mariah looked dejected. "What are we going to do?"

21   Laura spun around slowly, trying to come up with something. "I know! Follow me!" She grabbed Mariah's hand and pulled her along. "We can climb the oak tree two houses down. If we get high enough, we'll have a perfect view!"

22   Mariah's face broke into a wide smile, and she nodded. She and Laura rushed over to the tree. Laura made a basket with her hands and boosted Mariah up to the first branch. Then she jumped and followed Mariah up until they found a wide, comfortable branch to perch on.

23   Mariah giggled. "Look at us! We're like jaguars."

24   Laura grinned and said, "Yeah! Jaguars about to see the Queen."

25   Then they heard the roar of the crowd. The parade had started, and the Queen was on her way.

Comprehension Check

1. Reread paragraph 5. What comparison is being made in this paragraph through figurative language?

    a. A comparison of Mariah's eyes and two stars

    b. A comparison of two stars with each other

    c. A comparison of Mariah's eyes and excitement

    d. A comparison of two stars and excitement

2. If this were a play, how many scenes would it have?

    a. 1

    b. 2

    c. 3

    d. 4

3. How do the pronouns and descriptive words in the story help you understand Laura and Mariah's point of view about seeing the Queen of England? How would you feel about fighting the crowd for a view of the Queen?

The pronouns and discribtibs tell us that the you and shows to bt excited girls wonted

4. Put a star by the example of figurative language in paragraph 12. How does this language emphasize the characters' feelings? Support your answer with text evidence.

She is worred and upset that they dod't get to see the queen

RL.9, SL.3.1a, SL.3.1.c, SL.3.1.d, SL.3.4

Compare and Contrast Texts

In this unit, you have read four stories about friendship. You learned about relationships between people and service dogs, between two boys, between a boy and a girl, and between two girls in Victorian England. Now, pick out two of the four texts you read for this unit. Using the Venn diagram below, map out what the stories have in common and what is unique about them. Think about the ways friendship is presented in each text. Be prepared to discuss your ideas.

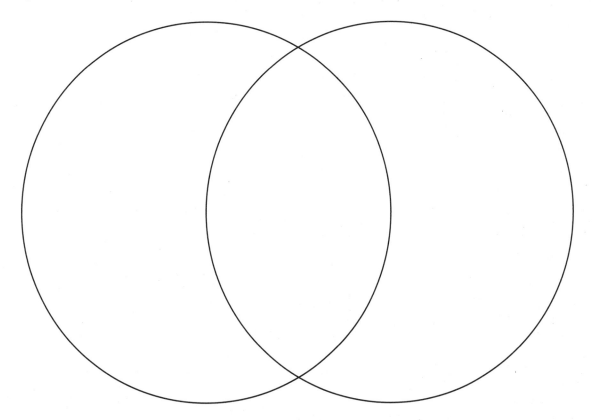

Return to the Essential Question

How do authors craft stories?

In small groups or as a class, discuss the Essential Question. Think about what you have learned about figurative language, sections of a text (like scenes or chapters), and point of view. Use evidence from the four unit texts to answer the question.

Literal and Nonliteral Meanings

L.3.5.a

Guided Instruction **Nonliteral**, or **figurative**, language is language that means something other than what the words say.

An idiom is an example of figurative language. Idioms are popular expressions that have been used for a long time. The meaning of an idiom can be much different from the literal meanings of its words. Read this sentence from "We Must See the Queen!": *Keeping their shortcut a secret would be a piece of cake*. The idiom *that's a piece of cake* means "that is really easy."

bend over backwards	1. nonliteral meaning: to do whatever is needed to help
	2. literal meaning: to completely bend one's back
a green thumb	1. nonliteral meaning: someone good at gardening
	2. literal meaning: someone's thumb is the color green

Look at the chart to find other examples of nonliteral idiomatic phrases.

Guided Practice Determine whether each sentence uses an idiom or not. In the blank before each sentence, write "n" for *nonliteral* or "l" for *literal* meaning.

_____ **1.** As he painted, he saw that he had a green thumb.

_____ **2.** Look at her garden; she has a real green thumb.

_____ **3.** His mom bent over backwards to make his birthday happy.

_____ **4.** She had to bend over backwards to get under the fence.

Independent Practice Using the phrase *hold on to your hat*, write one sentence that contains an idiom, or nonliteral meaning, and one that contains a literal meaning.

_____

_____

_____

_____

RL.3.4, RL.3.5, RL.3.6, L.3.5.a

Read the following passage in which nonliteral language and a narrator's point of view appear in the stanzas of a poem. Then answer the questions on pages 125 and 126.

Friendship—Yum

(Genre: poem)

1 What does the word *friendship*
  Mean to you?
  Is it about being faithful
  To friends pure and true?
  Does it mean trusting others
  With all your might?
  Does it mean always agreeing
  With never a fight?

2 I think friendship's like chocolate
  And fruit combined.
  It's delicious and nutritious,
  And sometimes it's mine.
  Look out for nice friends,
  And if a fine one you meet,
  Hold on; a great friendship
  Is good enough to eat.

Fill in the circle of the correct answer choice.

1. Which word in stanza 2 shows the opinion belongs to the narrator?

   ● I

   ○ delicious

   ○ nice

   ○ you

2. In which stanza of the poem does the narrator compare friendship to food?

   ○ stanza 1

   ● stanza 2

UNIT 5 COMMON CORE REVIEW

RL.3.4, RL.3.5, RL.3.6, L.3.5.a

3. If the poem was instead a drama, what part of a drama would stanza 1 be?

- ● dialogue
- ○ setting
- ○ characters
- ○ stage directions

4. Which word in stanza 2 hints that figurative language will follow?

- ○ it's
- ○ fine
- ○ good
- ● like

5. Underline the nonliteral language in stanza 2.

6. Write what the author means by the idiom "Hold on."

The author means to hold on your friendship.

7. Select one idea about friendship from the poem. Rewrite the idea using figurative or nonliteral language.

Look out for nice friends, And if a fine one you meet.

8. How does the point of view change from stanza 1 to 2?

The change is in stanza 1 it is asking you quesions. In stanza 2 it is telling you advice.

9. What is the narrator's point of view about friendship?

The narrator's point of view about friendship is that keep your friendship.

10. Do you share the narrator's point of view on friendship?

I do share the narrator's point of view on friendship.

Unit 5 ■ Reading Literature: Craft and Structure

Introducing UNIT 6

In this unit about friendship, you will learn how to write a nonfictional narrative. A nonfictional narrative is a story about a real experience or event.

When you write a nonfictional narrative, you want to carefully think about the event sequence. The story is told in the order it happened. As a writer, you will include a beginning, middle, and end.

When writing, you will want to choose words and phrases carefully. Use dialogue and descriptions to explain the experience. Connect events using time-order words. Your nonfictional narrative should also be grammatically correct.

Before Unit 6

Progress Check *Can I?*

After Unit 6

- [ ] Sequence my nonfictional narrative with a beginning, middle, and end. [ ]
- [ ] Write using descriptive details. [ ]
- [ ] Write using time-order words to show the order of events. [ ]
- [ ] Use dialogue to develop events. [ ]
- [ ] Write using the correct tense of a verb. [ ]
- [ ] Write using regular and irregular verbs. [ ]
- [ ] Write using correct subject-verb agreement. [ ]
- [ ] Spell correctly when adding suffixes to base words. [ ]

HOME◆CONNECT...

- Learn to write a nonfictional narrative using dialogue, descriptive details, and a clear sequence of events.

- Learn to use time-order words such as *next, then,* and *last* to show the order of events.

- Learn specific language skills and use them in writing a nonfictional narrative:

  - Write verbs to show actions in the narrative.

  - Use the correct verb tense to show when the action happened.

  - Correctly use regular and irregular verbs such as *I* blow *a bubble* and *I* blew *a bubble.*

  - Use correct singular and plural subject-verb agreement.

  - Recognize suffixes that change the meaning of a base word.

NOTE: All of these learning goals for your child are based on the Grade 3 Common Core State Standards for English Language Arts.

In this unit, children will learn to write about real events and experiences as part of the **nonfictional narrative** form. Explain that many people enjoy recording their experiences in diaries, journals, or blogs. These can be records of special events and exeriences. Encourage your child to retell the events of a special experience, such as a trip to the zoo or losing a tooth.

When writing a nonfictional narrative, your child will be asked to **sequence events** in the order they occurred. As your child retells a special event, ask: *What happened first? What happened next? What happened last?* Help your child think of some **descriptive details** about his or her special event. Ask what was said during the event. This will add **dialogue** and interest to your child's narrative. Encourage him or her to **provide a good ending** by explaining what made the event special and how he or she felt.

On the Go: Show your child examples of child-friendly blogs—perhaps a travel blog or movie blog for family movies. Then, ask your child to write about his or her experiences. Encourage him or her to select one important recent event. If you wish, ask your child to share the blog with family or friends who don't live nearby.

WAYS TO HELP YOUR CHILD

Discuss special events with your child. For example, instead of telling about the weekend, encourage your child just to tell about dinner at Grandma's. Ask questions: *What did it look like? How did you feel?* Descriptive details add to the event.

> ONLINE
>
> **For more Home Connect activities, continue online at** sadlierconnect.com

Text Types and Purposes: Write Nonfictional Narratives

UNIT 6

Essential Question:
How do writers develop nonfictional narratives?

W.3.3.a, W.3.3.b

CREATING AN ORGANIZATIONAL STRUCTURE

Abbey used an outline to organize her nonfictional narrative. It divides the sequence of events into three sections: beginning, middle, and end.

Title: _____
Characters: _____

Story Events:

Beginning:

Middle:

End:

EVENT SEQUENCE

- The beginning of the narrative introduces the event and the narrator.

- It uses words for effect and gets the reader's attention.

Underline a sentence that tells what happened at the beginning.

Read a Student Model

Abbey is in the third grade. She has been asked to write a nonfictional narrative about a special day with a friend. She has been asked to use a clear event sequence and to describe her thoughts, feelings, and actions. As you read her nonfictional narrative, think about what event you will share and what words you will use to describe the event.

A Hand to Help

Lots of colored balloons clung to the ceiling. Loudspeakers blared my favorite music. It was a party, so why was I sitting in the middle of the floor crying? It was a skating party, and I had never been on skates before.

My mom had carefully fastened my bubblegum-pink skates. She turned around to help my little brother with his black ones. I tried to stand up, but instead I wobbled and fell on the shiny hardwood floor. My knees buckled and my hands stung as I tried to break my fall. I felt embarrassed.

W.3.3.a–c

As I watched my friends skating effortlessly around and around the rink, I wanted to crawl into a hole. Emma waved from across the room. "Oh no! She's coming over here," I thought.

Emma glided to a graceful stop in front of me. I peeked up at her. She had a big smile on her face.

"Would you like to go for a spin?" she asked.

I shook my head no. She tried to bend down closer but lost her balance. Her hands were flying around as she tried to break her fall. Then she ended up on the floor just like me.

Emma laughed. "I think I spend more time falling than I do skating!"

"At least you can stand up. I can't skate at all," I replied.

"You will, too. We'll hold onto the rail until you can go on your own."

Having a friend by my side gave me a lot of confidence. I grabbed the rail and Emma's hand in a tight grip as I slowly pulled myself off the floor. I wobbled but eventually managed to stand on my own two feet. In the beginning, I held on to the rail and pulled myself along.

DIALOGUE AND DESCRIPTIONS

- Dialogue shows thoughts and feelings of characters.
- Descriptions give details about how things look, smell, sound, or feel.

Underline descriptive words in the first paragraph on this page that show how the narrator feels.

Put a star next to Emma's first line of dialogue.

EVENT SEQUENCE

The middle of the nonfictional narrative continues the sequence of events in the order they happened.

TIME-ORDER WORDS AND PHRASES

Words such as *before*, *until*, and *eventually* tell when events happen. Use time-order words and phrases to signal the order of events and make the event sequence clear.

Circle words that show the sequence of events.

PROVIDE A STRONG ENDING

The ending tells how the events worked out or how the writer felt about the events.

Underline the words that Abbey used to signal the ending.

Then, I released my grip on the rail but my hand stayed close to it.

By the end of the party, I was skating around and around with everyone else. It was so much fun to glide and coast. It felt a little like flying. I felt brave for trying something new and scary. I couldn't have done it without my friend. Emma never left my side. She helped me laugh when I would get upset. She cheered me on when I was doing well. It wasn't learning to skate that made the day special. It was learning what a great friend Emma had been to me.

W.3.3.a-d, W.3.4, W.3.5, W.3.10

Use an organizer like Abbey's to plan your own nonfictional narrative about a special day with a friend. Then write a first draft of your story on a separate piece of paper. Don't forget to use dialogue, descriptions, and time-order words in your narrative. You will use this draft to write your final story draft in the Common Core Review section on page 140.

Title: The shoping day with my cousin

Characters: Samantha, Angela, YiYi, and Mom

Story Events:

Beginning: One day, I had nothing to do until I heard my mom say "Sam we are going to see Angela" Yay I shoted with joy!

Middle: Then Angela Mom drive to our house and we went inside her car and we drove up to payless then we went to other stores

End: After that we went to the market and there were blue boxes. Everything else was white. We were playing a game that you have to step on the blue boxes.

L.3.1.a, L.3.1.e

Verbs and Verb Tenses

Guided Instruction A **verb tense** tells when an action happens. When an action happens now or regularly, the verb is in the **present tense**.

*Kylie **visits** Beth at her house.*
*Kylie and Sarah **visit** Beth at her house.*

When an action has already happened, the verb is in the *past tense*.

*Last week, Kylie **visited** Beth at her house.*

When an action is going to happen, the verb is in the *future tense*.

*Tomorrow, Kylie **will visit** Beth at her house.*

Guided Practice Write the correct tense of the word in parentheses.

1. Today, I _____ walked _____ to Tom's house. (walk)

2. Yesterday, I _____ walk + _____ to Tom's house. (walk)

3. Tomorrow, I _____ will walk _____ to Tom's house. (walk)

4. Every month, I _____ walk _____ to Tom's house. (walk)

Independent Practice Use the correct tense of the verb in parentheses to complete each sentence.

1. The friends _____ work _____ on a group project right now. (work)

2. The group _____ talked _____ about the plans a month ago. (talk)

3. They _____ started _____ it yesterday. (start)

4. Tomorrow, the boys and girls _____ will look _____ for poster board and paints. (look)

5. They _____ will finished _____ the project next week. (finish)

L.3.1.d

Regular and Irregular Verbs

Guided Instruction Most verbs form the past tense by adding *-ed* to the end. **Irregular verbs** change their spelling when forming the past tense.

work (regular verb)	worked	We **worked** on the group project last night.
come (irregular verb)	came	We **came** home late.

Guided Practice Underline the verb that correctly completes the sentence.

1. Two friends (goed, went) to the park.

2. They (brought, bringed) a picnic lunch.

3. After they (eated, ate), they threw away the trash.

4. Then they (took, taked) the water bottles home.

Independent Practice Write the correct past tense of the verbs in parentheses on the line.

1. Arjun ____ran____ the race last week. (run)

2. Arjun's friend ____broke____ his leg. (break)

3. Arjun ____pushed____ his friend in a wheelchair. (push)

4. They____knew____ how to finish the race. (know)

5. Their parents ____came____ to watch. (come)

6. The crowd ____saw____ a great race. (see)

Subject-Verb Agreement

Guided Instruction The subject and verb in a sentence must both be singular or both be plural.

- If the subject is a singular noun or pronoun, add -s to the verb.

    The **lizard runs** across the sand.

- If the subject is a plural noun or pronoun, do not add -s to the verb.

    The **lizards run** across the sand.

Guided Practice Write the word in parentheses that correctly completes each sentence.

1. Many animals _____live_____ on or around the cactus. (live, lives)
2. The wren _____makes_____ a nest on the branch. (make, makes)
3. The _____owl_____ hunts at night. (owl, owls)
4. Some _____insects_____ eat cactus. (insect, insects)

Independent Practice Correct the mistakes in subject-verb agreement. Write the new sentences.

1. The woodpecker make a hole in the cactus.

    _____

2. Inside the nest, the babies sleeps safely.

    _____

3. When the babies leave, other birds uses the nest.

    _____

4. A woodpecker eat insects.

    _____

5. Gila woodpeckers lives as long as 10 years.

    _____

L.3.2.e

Suffixes

Guided Instruction A **suffix** is a word part that is added to the end of a word to change its meaning. Suffixes can be added to the end of verbs to change them into a different part of speech. Sometimes the spelling of the base word is changed when a suffix is added. Here the *e* is dropped before adding *-ing*.

*I like to **bake** cookies.*
*Mom likes **baking** pies in the winter.*

Suffixes can also be added to nouns and adjectives to change their meaning. When a base word ends in *y* preceded by a consonant, the *y* changes to *i* before the suffix is added.

*What makes you feel **happy**?*
*I feel **happiness** when I play at the park with friends.*

Guided Practice Add the suffix to the base word and spell the new word on the line.

1. shop + er_____

2. cute + est_____

3. penny + less_____

4. silly + est_____

Independent Practice Complete each sentence with the correct base word and suffix.

1. He is the_____ person I know. (brave + est)

2. The child picked up the_____ on the floor. (wrap + er)

3. Liam's hair was _____ than any I've ever seen! (curly + er)

4. Joni would_____ help the young child. (happy + ly)

5. Rene was a _____ in the ice show. (skate + er)

Discuss the Essential Question

How do writers develop nonfictional narratives?

Think about the Essential Question by responding to the questions below. Support your point of view with details from Abbey's story.

1. What words does the writer use to signal the order of the story?

_____

2. What are some words or phrases the writer uses to describe events?

_____

_____

_____

Use your notes above to discuss the Essential Question in small groups or as a class. Follow agreed-upon rules for discussion. Use the organizer below to record what you heard and how you participated.

	Ideas I Agree or Disagree With	Questions I Asked
Agree		
Disagree		
	New Ideas I Had During Discussion	**Questions I Answered**

L.3.1.a, L.3.1.d–f, L.3.2.e

This paragraph has mistakes in the use of regular and irregular verb tenses, subject-verb agreement, as well as suffixes. Write the paragraph correctly on the lines below. Use a dictionary to help you spell the words.

Last week, Kate and I had a lemonade stand. We want to raise money for the hospital that is careing for our sick friend. First, we will ask our parents for permission. Then, we puts together our supplies. Kate mixes the lemonade, and I carefully poured it into the glasses. We selled the tastyest lemonade ever for fifty cents. At the end of the day, we raised twenty dollars. It gave us both great happyness to help our friend.

_____

_____

_____

_____

_____

_____

_____

_____

_____

_____

_____

W.3.3.a–d, W.3.4, W.3.5, W.3.10

Assignment: Write a nonfictional narrative about a special day with a friend.

On the lines below, write your final copy of the nonfictional narrative draft you created on page 133. Be sure to describe your thoughts, feelings, and actions. Make sure to choose your words carefully and use words to signal the order of events. You may also use dialogue to explain events and tell about the characters. Wrap up your narrative with a conclusion. See the Writing Handbook (pp. 275–283) for ways to improve your writing as you revise.

_____

_____

_____

_____

_____

_____

_____

_____

_____

_____

_____

_____

_____

_____

_____

There are three parts to this performance task. Your teacher will provide you with copies of three reading selections.

- "The Missing Glove"   Genre: Realistic Fiction
- "A Famous Voyage to Antarctica"   Genre: Historical Narrative
- "Continent of Ice"   Genre: Informational Text

Part 1: Literary Analysis

☐ Read "The Missing Glove" carefully. Take notes that will help you understand the passage.

☐ Answer Items 1–3 on pages 142–143.

☐ Then read the prompt for Item 4 and write a paragraph on your own paper. You may want to make some notes on scratch paper first.

Part 2: Narrative Writing

☐ Read "A Famous Voyage to Antarctica" carefully. Take notes that will help you understand the passage.

☐ Answer Items 1–2 on page 144.

☐ Then read the prompt for Item 3 and write two or three paragraphs on your own paper. You may want to make some notes on scratch paper first.

Part 3: Research Simulation

☐ Read "Continent of Ice" carefully. Take notes that will help you understand the passage.

☐ Answer Items 1–3 about "Continent of Ice" on pages 145–146.

☐ Review "A Famous Voyage to Antarctica." You will use it in addition to "Continent of Ice" in this task.

☐ Then read the prompt for Item 4 and write an essay on your own paper. You may want to make some notes on scratch paper first.

RL.3.1, RL.3.3, RL.3.4, RL.3.10, W.3.2, W.3.4, W.3.10, L.3.1, L.3.2, L.3.4.a

Part 1 Literary Analysis

Read all parts of the question before responding. Circle the correct answers to Items 1–3. Use your own paper to respond to Item 4.

Item 1

Part A   In the story "The Missing Glove," what makes Dr. Lin so upset?

a. She receives special clothes for very cold weather.

b. She loses a piece of gear that is very important.

c. She thinks that no one remembers it is her birthday.

d. She hasn't seen flowers in her six months in Antarctica.

Part B   Which sentence from the story best supports the answer to Part A?

a. "The government has issued her all the items . . . "

b. "Every Antarctica worker got the same items."

c. "Dr. Lin started feeling more and more anxious."

d. "She could not perform her work without that glove . . ."

Item 2

Part A   In the story "The Missing Glove," what happens that makes Dr. Lin feel warm and happy?

a. Her friends surprise her by turning away when they see her.

b. Her friends surprise her with flowers for her birthday.

c. Her friends surprise her by putting her glove in the refrigerator.

d. Her friends surprise her with a new glove made just for her.

Part B Which detail from the story best supports the answer to Part A?

a. It is the first time she has seen a flower in the six months she has been in Antarctica.

b. It is a shock to find her glove because it is in the kitchen refrigerator.

c. It is unusual that her friends turn away and then yell, "Surprise!"

d. It is a comfort to find the lost glove so that she can do her work.

Item 3

Part A What does the word *extremely* mean in this line from "The Missing Glove"?

"She was *extremely* careful to keep track of it all."

a. briefly

b. easily

c. gently

d. very

Part B Which sentence from the story best helps the reader understand the meaning of *extremely*?

a. "She was nearing the end of her six-month job . . . "

b. "She worked outside . . . "

c. "She even kept a detailed checklist."

d. "She also got hats, hoods, and goggles."

Item 4

Think about how Dr. Lin's feelings change throughout the story. How does she feel at the end of the story? How are her feelings at the end of the story different from those at the beginning? Write a paragraph to explain your answer. Use details from the story to support your answer.

NARRATIVE WRITING

RI.3.2, RI.3.10, W.3.3, W.3.4,
W.3.10, L.3.1, L.3.2, L.3.4.a

Part 2 Narrative Writing

Read all parts of the question before responding. Circle the correct answers to Items 1–2. Use your own paper to respond to Item 3.

Item 1

Part A What is the main idea of "A Famous Voyage to Antarctica"?

a. Sir Ernest Shackleton never reached the South Pole.

b. Exploring Antarctica is too dangerous and shouldn't be tried.

c. Iron ships are better for Antarctic expeditions than wooden ones.

d. The crew of the *Endurance* survived two years trapped in ice.

Part B Which text detail does NOT support the answer to Part A?

a. "Shackleton made four trips to the frozen continent."

b. "They would not return to civilization for two long years."

c. "If they survived the trip, they would return with help."

d. "Not a single life had been lost."

Item 2

Part A What is the meaning of *hazardous* in this sentence from the text?

"Men wanted for *hazardous* journey."

a. calm   b. unsafe   c. exciting   d. enjoyable

Part B Which detail helps readers understand the meaning of *hazardous*?

a. Many men applied to be on the *Endurance* crew.

b. Shackleton was buried on South Georgia Island.

c. The crew had to camp on an ice floe for many months.

d. Shackleton's advertisement warned of "constant danger."

Item 3

Think about the events described in "A Famous Voyage to Antarctica." Then write two paragraphs to tell what might have happened to the last crew members to be rescued from Elephant Island. Use ideas and facts from "A Famous Voyage to Antarctica" to help your writing.

RI.3.2, RI.3.4, RI.3.5, RI.3.9, RI.3.10, W.3.2, W.3.4, W.3.7, W.3.8, W.3.10, L.3.1, L.3.2, L.3.4.a

Part 3 Research Simulation

Read all parts of the question before responding. Circle the correct answers to Items 1–3. Use your own paper to respond to Item 4.

Item 1

Part A In "Continent of Ice," where would the reader find facts about things scientists can learn in Antarctica?

a. in the first paragraph

b. in "What Is Antarctica Like?"

c. in "Who Lives in Antarctica?"

d. in "Why Do Scientists Study in Antarctica?"

Part B Which sentence from the text best supports the answer to Part A?

a. "Antarctica covers Earth's South Pole."

b. "Antarctica is the coldest place on Earth."

c. "Antarctica is a good place to find meteorites . . . "

d. "Antarctica has no trees or bushes."

Item 2

Part A What does the text say that scientists might find out about from studying Antarctica?

a. deserts

b. Mars

c. many types of whales

d. seals and penguins

Part B Which details from the text best support the answer to Part A?

a. Antarctica has a warmer temperature on its coasts than at its center.

b. Antarctica has only moss and algae for plants.

c. Antarctica has meteorites, or rocks from space.

d. Antarctica has cold weather and is dry like Mars.

Item 3

Part A   What does the word *analyze* mean in this part of "Continent of Ice"?

"Also, meteorites that fall in Antarctica are protected by the ice for a long time. This gives scientists more time to *analyze* them in order to learn more about these rocks."

a. to clean something well

b. to do something quickly

c. to study something carefully

d. to keep something cold

Part B   Which set of words from the passage best help the reader understand the meaning of *analyze* in Part A?

a. protected; ice; long time

b. scientists; more time; learn

c. in order; more; these rocks

d. that fall; protected; gives

Item 4

You have read two texts describing Antarctica. Think about the facts in "A Famous Voyage to Antarctica" and the facts in "Continent of Ice." What challenges do people face when they are working and exploring in Antarctica? Write a paragraph to explain how these challenges affect people. Use details from the passages to support your answer.

Introducing UNIT 7

In this unit about extreme weather, you will learn about what makes up craft and structure in informational text. Craft and structure refers to the tools that authors use to create a text.

When you read a magazine article or a history book, you are reading informational text. This unit deals with a science topic. Authors may use words that you do not know in their explanations of scientific ideas. Knowing how to figure out or find the meanings of words you do not know is especially important to understanding what you read. Authors of informational text may also use text features, such as sidebars and hyperlinks, to present ideas. It's important to know how to use these sources of information.

Thinking about an author's point of view and the way that the author uses words and language can also help you understand what you read. You will learn more about this and the other tools as you complete this unit.

Progress Check *Can I?*

Before Unit 7 ☐ — **After Unit 7** ☐

☐ Determine the meaning of academic and content area words and phrases. ☐

☐ Use text features and search tools to locate information. ☐

☐ Distinguish my point of view from the author's point of view. ☐

☐ Find the meaning of a new word when a familiar prefix or suffix is added. ☐

HOME◆CONNECT...

Newspaper writers and editors are good about providing context clues for tough words in their articles. **Context clues** are words that give readers the help they need to understand the meanings of unfamiliar words. Choose a print or online news article your child might enjoy. Highlight any difficult words defined in context. Then ask your child to help you use context clues to find the meanings of the highlighted words.

Text features such as subheads, charts, and sidebars can help children see what is important in an article. Choose an online article with an appealing topic. Before reading, have your child point out subheads and predict what the article will be about. Talk about sidebars, maps, and charts, and discuss why information is shown this way.

Understanding an **author's point of view** about a subject is an important reading skill. Find an editorial in a newspaper or children's magazine. Read it with your child. Have your child state the author's opinion and say whether they agree with the author.

Activity: With your child, explore interesting Web links related to extreme weather. Use correct terms for the text features you see on screen, such as *sidebar, heading, caption, hyperlink, boldface type*. Talk about why some of the texts you explore are easier to follow or more appealing than others. List the interesting new facts you learn, and create your own fact sheet on the computer.

IN THIS UNIT, YOUR CHILD WILL...

- Use clues in a text to figure out the meaning of unfamiliar words and words with multiple meanings.

- Learn how text features such as headings or visuals (charts, photos, hyperlinks, etc.) help readers locate information within the text.

- Identify an author's point of view, or opinion, about a topic, and decide whether or not he or she agrees with it.

- Combine the meaning of a base word, such as *agree*, with those of prefixes and suffixes, such as *dis-* and *-able*, to understand word meanings.

- Compare and contrast four texts on the same theme: an explanatory text, a magazine article, an editorial, and a personal narrative.

NOTE: All of these learning goals for your child are based on the Grade 3 Common Core State Standards for English Language Arts.

WAYS TO HELP YOUR CHILD

Show respect for your child's point of view on topics while also helping your child develop the thinking and speaking skills needed to express and support opinions. Whether you are discussing sports, current events, or daily life, ask for your child's point of view. Encourage him or her to offer supporting reasons for it.

ONLINE

For more Home Connect activities, continue online at sadlierconnect.com

Reading Informational Text: Craft and Structure

Essential Question:
How can authors present informational text effectively?

Guided Instruction

RI.3.4

WORDS TO KNOW

barrier
levee
system

> To determine the **meaning of a word**, readers can use context clues located in the same sentence as the word or in nearby sentences.

CITE EVIDENCE

A Inference clues help you figure out the **meaning of an unknown word**. By using the text, readers can infer—or figure out—what a word means. Circle the word *submerged* in paragraph 2. Underline the nearby words that help you figure out its meaning.

B Synonyms are words that have the same or similar meanings, such as *big/large*. Sometimes synonyms can be context clues. Circle the word *halt* and its synonym in the last sentence of paragraph 3. Why are synonyms often good context clues?

Water Everywhere
(Genre: Explanatory Text)

1   The worst flood in the United States took place in 1993. It is known as "The Great Flood of 1993." It rained for five months, causing the Mississippi and Missouri rivers to overflow. This extra water resulted in flooding across nine states.

Too Much Rain

2   **Levees** stand along the sides of the rivers and keep the river water from going into nearby towns. This time, there was too much rain. Water went over the first **barrier** on June 7. Seventy-five towns were soon submerged. Garbage, bridge parts, and lumber floated on the river. The river water even lifted entire houses.

Floods in the Future

3   We can protect ourselves from floods. Better levees can be built to hold back floodwaters. Rainfall can be measured by taking pictures from space. A flood warning **system** is also important. It can send an alert to people to leave their homes. Human beings can't stop the rain, but we may be able to halt its flow.

RI.3.4

4   Flooding is a big problem in places that are below sea level. The Netherlands is a country in Europe. That country has been dealing with floods for a long time. And people there have some new ideas.

Fighting Floods

5   In the Netherlands, the Dutch fight floods by letting some water in. As sea levels rise, levees and other barriers do not work as well. So the Dutch government created a flood zone. Floodwaters can spill there. No one is hurt. No property is damaged.

6   In the United States, during Hurricane Katrina in 2005, the levees around New Orleans failed. The city was badly flooded. New levees kept the city mostly dry during Hurricane Isaac in 2012, but other areas were swamped. It may not be possible to protect everyone with levees. The East Coast also experienced massive flooding in 2012 during Hurricane Sandy. Now some people there are wondering if they should create flood zones as people have done in the Netherlands.

CITE EVIDENCE

C Restatement occurs when a text restates what a word means—similar to a definition. Sentence 3 in paragraph 5 includes the term *flood zone*. Underline the restatement that helps you figure out the meaning of *flood zone*. How does the restatement help you?

D Antonyms are words that are opposite in meaning, like *glad/sad.* Sometimes antonyms can be used as context clues. Circle the word *swamped* and its antonym in paragraph 6.

Comprehension Check

How does determining the meaning of *flood zone* help you understand solutions to flooding? Give specific examples.

Water Everywhere *continued*

RI.3.4

WORDS TO KNOW

debris
disaster

CITE EVIDENCE

A Underline the words in paragraph 7 that help you determine what the word *dampness* means.

B Read paragraph 8. Circle the text that helps explain the word *assistance*. In paragraph 9, underline the context clue that helps you figure out what the word *strike* means.

Flood and Funds

7   Floods are expensive. Floodwater is powerful, lifting buildings off the ground and sending cars sailing. Floodwater is also dirty. When the water drains away from buildings, mud and other **debris** are left behind. The dirty water can ruin furniture, electrical appliances, and other household items. Dampness left behind by water causes mold to grow, and wood and other building materials can be ruined by water. Even a few inches of water can mean thousands of dollars in cleaning and repairs. Many buildings cannot be repaired.

8   A major flood can cost billions of dollars. After Hurricane Sandy, some neighborhoods were completely destroyed. New York City subway tunnels were underwater. That flood was a **disaster**, and many people needed assistance. Government workers rescued those who were stranded. They provided food and water. The government also gave people money to fix their homes and businesses.

Finding Solutions

9   Floods can strike almost anywhere. But they tend to hit the same places over and over. Low-lying places near water are at the greatest risk. People build homes where there may be floods. When a flood hits, they may get money from the government to rebuild. Sometimes they rebuild in the same spot.

10   Some say these owners should be allowed to rebuild where they want. It's their home. Others say that when government pays, everyone pays. They think the owners should not be allowed to rebuild in the same place. What do you think?

Comprehension Check

1. Circle the letter next to the word that helps you figure out the meaning of *appliances* in paragraph 7.

a. dirty

b. ruin

c. furniture

d. electrical

2. Circle the letter next to the word that is a synonym of *provided* in paragraph 8.

a. rescued

b. stranded

c. gave

d. fix

3. Work with a partner to determine the meanings of unknown words on pages 152–153. Why is it important to know what the words mean in order to understand information in the passage?

It is iportant to understand the meanings
of words to understand the story

_____

_____

_____

DETERMINING WORD MEANINGS

RI.3.4

WORDS TO KNOW
absorb
contaminated
snowmelt

CITE EVIDENCE

A Circle an antonym that helps you determine the meaning of the word *treacherous* in the first sentence of paragraph 13.

B In paragraph 13, bullet point 3, underline a synonym for *evacuate*. How did these synonyms and antonyms help you understand this section on flood safety?

Water Everywhere *continued*

What Causes Floods?

11   Floods are caused by storms and heavy rain. But other conditions cause flooding as well. Melting snow can turn into gallons of water. **Snowmelt** can flow downhill and fill rivers and streams. When they get too full, they overflow. Wildfires can also lead to flooding. Fire burns away the trees and other plants that **absorb** water. Without plants to soak up the water, floodwaters take longer to go down.

12   Finally, dam failures also cause floods. Dams control the flow of rivers. They can create lakes that we use for fun or to supply us with drinking water. Dams can also turn the flow of water into a source of electrical power. But if a dam fails, all that water rushes out, crushing everything in its path. The floodwater from a dam break is like a tidal wave because the water moves with great force. A dam failure was the cause of the tragic Johnstown flood in Pennsylvania. It happened in 1889 after heavy rains. More than 2,200 people died.

Flood Safety

13   Floods can be treacherous. Take steps to stay safe.

- Listen to the weather forecast if you are at risk. A flood watch means a flood is possible. A flood warning means flooding has begun.
- Unplug electrical appliances.
- If you are asked to evacuate, leave as quickly as you can. Keep a bag packed with essential items that you can grab fast.
- Do not try to walk through moving water. It can knock you down. And floodwater can be **contaminated** with waste.

14   After a flood you may need to boil water to make it safe to drink. Be sure electrical appliances are completely dry before you use them. Watch out for snakes or other creatures that might have floated into your home. Floods are the most common natural disaster. So stay safe!

Comprehension Check   MORE ONLINE   sadlierconnect.com

1. Circle the letter next to the word in paragraph 13 that helps you figure out the meaning of the word *contaminated.*

   a. float

   (b. waste)

   c. water

   d. flood

2. Circle the letter next to the words in paragraph 11 that help you determine the meaning of the word *overflow.*

   (a. get too full)

   b. gallons of water

   c. flow downhill

   d. fill rivers and streams

3. The section "What Causes Floods?" discusses the conditions that bring about flooding. What context clues tell you the meaning of *conditions* in paragraph 11? How does knowing the meaning of the word help you understand this section?

   condisin can help explane what helps floding

USING TEXT FEATURES

Guided Instruction

RI.3.5

WORDS TO KNOW
atmosphere
destroy

Text features and search tools help readers locate information.

CITE EVIDENCE

A A **hyperlink** is a search tool that is used to find **information** on the Internet. The words in the link tell what information can be found there when you click on it. Circle the hyperlink in paragraph 1. Underline the word that tells what information you might find when you click on it.

B A **subhead** is a title within a selection. This text feature introduces a specific part of a reading passage. Subheads are included on a separate line above the part of the passage they introduce. Put a star next to the subhead on this page. What might you learn in this section?

Watch Out for Weather!
(Genre: Journal Article)

1   Tornadoes, hurricanes, and blizzards are all extreme weather events. They are often called natural disasters. Scientists at the National Weather Service (**www.weather.gov**) watch and study weather. They warn people when a dangerous storm is on its way. Each year, the National Weather Service sends out 50,000 warnings for extreme weather events. The warnings give people time to prepare for storms and protect themselves.

Twirling Tornadoes

2   *Twister, funnel,* and *whirlwind* are all nicknames for one dangerous weather event: a tornado. Tornadoes develop from thunderstorms. Before a tornado appears, warm air near the ground meets cold air higher in the **atmosphere**. The two masses of air push against each other in a circular motion. Then they form a funnel of water droplets. If the funnel touches the ground, the storm is a tornado. Winds inside a tornado may reach 200 miles per hour. The funnel picks up dust and dirt in its path. It can even uproot trees and pick up cars. One big tornado picked up a train. It carried the train in the air for 80 feet. All the passengers were still inside!

RI.3.5

3   Tornado funnels can be a mile wide. Most of them do not stay on the ground for long. Still, they do a lot of damage. Tornadoes can **destroy** everything in their paths. Hospitals, schools, and homes may be completely ruined. Because they twist and turn as they race across the ground, tornadoes may destroy one house and leave the next one untouched.

4   Sometimes a tornado travels over water. It forms a waterspout. It picks up water and fish along the way. Some fish have been carried hundreds of miles in water spouts.

TORNADO ALERT!

People may be injured or killed by objects tossed by the funnel. That is why it is important to know what to do when a tornado approaches.

- Stay inside.
- Go to the basement or ground floor.
- Stay away from windows.
- Get under a table or stairs that can protect you from falling objects.

CITE EVIDENCE

C A **sidebar** is a text feature that provides extra information about the topic of an article. Circle the "Tornado Alert!" sidebar.

D A **bulleted list** is a text feature that organizes information. A bullet is a small circle. Each bullet introduces a fact or piece of information. Put a star next to a bulleted piece of information about staying safe during a tornado. What else do you learn from this list?

Comprehension Check

How does each text feature in this passage improve your understanding of tornadoes?

This passage says that tornadoes can destroy everything in there paths

USING TEXT FEATURES

Watch Out for Weather! *continued*

RI.3.5

WORDS TO KNOW
crew
predict

CITE EVIDENCE

A Circle the text feature that gives you facts about hurricanes.

B Put a star next to the text feature that tells you that you will be reading about famous hurricanes.

C Underline the hyperlink. Why does the author include it?

Horrible Hurricanes

5   A hurricane can be as dangerous as a tornado. A hurricane is a storm that brings strong winds and heavy rain. Hurricanes begin as tropical storms near Earth's equator. They form over warm ocean waters. As the water becomes warmer, the winds become faster. Once wind speeds reach 75 miles per hour, the storm is a hurricane. The winds spin in a closed circle.

HURRICANE FACTS

- Hurricanes in the Pacific Ocean are usually called typhoons.
- Hurricanes in the Indian Ocean are usually called cyclones.
- When the eye of a hurricane passes overhead, the weather is sunny, calm, and quiet.
- Most hurricanes travel about 10–20 miles per hour.

Too Much Wind

6   Scientists on the ground need to get information about a storm. Hurricane hunters fly right into storms to get the facts. They bravely go into the storm's eye through fierce winds. The eye is the hurricane's calmest part. There the plane's **crew** drops instruments into the air. The instruments check wind speed and temperature. Scientists on the ground study the information and use it to **predict** how serious the storm will be. It's also important to try to figure out in what direction the storm will travel. Scientists can't stop a hurricane. But they can warn people who might be in the path of a natural disaster.

To see a video about hurricane hunters, visit **http://oceantoday.noaa.gov/hurricanehunters/ welcome.html**.

Famous Hurricanes

7 The Galveston hurricane hit Texas in 1900. Its highest winds reached 140 miles per hour. Hugo hit the Atlantic Coast in 1989. Its highest winds reached 160 miles per hour. Andrew hit Florida in 1992. Its highest winds reached 165 miles per hour. Katrina hit and destroyed much of New Orleans in 2005. Its highest winds reached 170 miles per hour.

Comprehension Check

1. Circle the letter next to the sentence that is NOT included in a sidebar text feature.

   a. Hurricanes in the Indian Ocean are usually called cyclones.

   b. Most hurricanes travel about 10–20 miles per hour.

   c. When the eye of a hurricane passes overhead, the weather is sunny, calm, and quiet.

   d. The Galveston hurricane hit Texas in 1900.

2. Circle the letter next to the text feature that a reader would use to see a video about hurricane hunters.

   a. Too Much Wind

   b. Hurricane Facts

   c. http://oceantoday.noaa.gov/hurricanehunters/welcome.html

   d. Famous Hurricanes

3. With a partner, read and discuss the "Hurricane Facts" sidebar on page 158. Why does the author include this text feature? How does it help you understand "Horrible Hurricanes"?

   It helps me understand Horrible Hurricanes
   by reading what i says a hurricane can be
   as dangerous as a tornado.

RI.3.5

WORDS TO KNOW

dangerous

prairie

severe

CITE EVIDENCE

A Under which subhead would you find information about blizzards in the Great Lakes area? Find that information and underline it.

B Underline the sentence in the text feature that states a fact about ground blizzards. What kind of text feature is inside the sidebar?

Watch Out for Weather! *continued*

What Is a Blizzard?

8   A blizzard is usually any serious snowstorm with strong winds of at least 35 miles per hour. To count as a blizzard, there has to be a lot of wind. While blizzards often mean lots of snow, there are no rules about how low the temperature has to be or how much snow must fall—if any—for a storm to be called a blizzard. **Severe** blizzards make it impossible to see buildings or trees just a few yards away.

9   Blizzards can be very **dangerous**. Since it is so hard to see outside, it is dangerous to travel. People can even get lost walking around their own backyard. Also, being out in cold temperatures and strong winds can cause frostbite, or frozen fingers and toes. Before weather could be predicted, blizzards could happen with almost no warning, such as when temperatures were warm. For an example, go to the link about the "Children's Blizzard" that happened in the late 1800s. **(http://www.farmersalmanac.com/weather/2012/01/09/the-childrens-blizzard/)**

Where and Why Do Blizzards Happen?

10   In North America, blizzards appear most in the **prairie** states, the Great Lakes, the northeastern United States, and Canada. Blizzards over the prairie happen when cold, dry northern air hits warm, wet southern air. In the Northeast, blizzards usually come from hurricanes moving down from the northern Atlantic Ocean. The poor Great Lakes area! It gets hit by both types of storms. This land is also affected by heavy lake snow and wind, which create even more chance of blizzards.

How to Prepare for a Blizzard

1¥   First, pay attention to the weather forecasts. Next, make sure you have flashlights, batteries, food, water, first aid supplies, and a backup heater in your home. Most importantly, stay inside!

BLIZZARD FACTS

- Some unusual blizzards bring no precipitation, or snow.
- Strong winds can pick up ground snow to create a "ground blizzard."
- The strength of a blizzard's wind is more important than the snowfall.

Comprehension Check

(MORE ONLINE) sadlierconnect.com

1. If you click the link mentioned in paragraph 9, you would expect to find information about

   a. a blizzard that happened without warning.

   b. children who played in the snow.

   c. the importance of having flashlights, batteries, and food.

   d. how farmers prepare for blizzards.

2. Circle the letter next to the sentence that is included in the sidebar.

   a. What is a blizzard?

   b. Some unusual blizzards bring no precipitation, or snow.

   c. Where and why do blizzards happen?

   d. Blizzards can be very dangerous.

3. Review the text features on pages 160–161. What did each text feature help you understand about blizzards? Cite text evidence to support your answer.

   Ih helps me orginize it!

Guided Instruction

RI.3.6

WORDS TO KNOW

condense

conserving

vapor

The author's **point of view** is the author's opinion on a topic. The reader can agree or disagree with this point of view.

CITE EVIDENCE

A In an editorial, the author's **point of view** is directly and clearly stated. Underline the sentence in paragraph 1 that states the author's point of view.

B The purpose of an editorial is to persuade the reader to share the author's point of view. To do this, the author gives evidence to support the opinion. Circle each fact in paragraph 1 that supports the author's point of view.

Stop the Droughts!
(Genre: Editorial)

1   Our state is currently in the middle of the third worst drought in history. Our land is drying up. Plants and animals are dying. People must change their behavior so that we can end this crisis soon.

2   Droughts happen when the earth is very dry. Because we depend on the water cycle to keep the earth wet, it's a problem when there is not enough rain. Things get worse when high temperatures dry out the land fast. Plants can't grow, and animals don't have enough to eat or drink. Without them, people have no food.

3   People can help lessen the effects of droughts by **conserving** water. We must always try to save water. Doing this before a problem arrives can help an area when it is hit by a drought. Here are a few things we can do to conserve water:

- Take shorter showers.
- Water lawns less often.
- Don't let faucets drip or run.

RI.3.6

4   It's essential to prepare for a drought. It's even more important to help keep droughts from coming in the first place. Earth is getting warmer. Cars and smokestacks burn fossil fuels, such as coal and oil. These fuels cause air pollution. The pollution traps heat in the atmosphere, affecting global climate.

5   We should care about global warming because higher temperatures help cause drought. In the water cycle, the sun causes water to evaporate into an invisible gas called water **vapor**. Cooler temperatures cause the vapor to **condense** and form rain. In an unusually hot area, the clouds take the water away. The water condenses and falls where the air is cooler. That is why droughts are worse in hotter areas.

Rules for Saving Water

6   Water conservation is more important than ever in places with low rainfall. The American Southwest has been suffering from major droughts for years. Many places have water restrictions that affect how often people can water gardens or fill their swimming pools.

7   Restrictions help save water for more important things, such as for drinking! Water conservation saves water for growing crops.

CITE EVIDENCE

C Often, an editorial asks the reader to take action. Underline the two sentences in paragraph 4 that tell the reader what he or she should do.

D Sometimes an author states opinions related to the main opinion. Circle the sentence that tells how the author feels about global warming. What information supports this point of view?

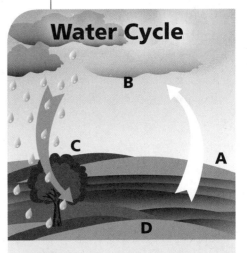

Water Cycle

A Evaporation—Sun turns water into steam.

B Condensation—Steam turns into liquid.

C Precipitation—Rain or snow falls.

D Collection—Water gathers in the ground or ocean.

Comprehension Check

What two weather-related reasons does the author give for drought? What is the author's point of view about the responsibility that people have to limit the effects of droughts? Cite text evidence in your answer.

DISTINGUISHING POINTS OF VIEW

Guided Practice

RI.3.6

WORDS TO KNOW
adapted
devastating

CITE EVIDENCE

A What does the author think you should care about in paragraph 8? Circle that piece of information.

B Put a star next to the evidence that the author gives in paragraph 9 to show that droughts are devastating. Explain to a partner why you do or do not share the author's point of view.

Stop the Droughts! *continued*

Drought and Famine Hurt Us All

8   Severe droughts are happening around the world. During a severe drought, the rainfall for the year remains less than average. If this goes on for years, reservoirs begin to dry up. Reservoirs are natural or human-made lakes that hold our drinking water. The plants and farm animals can die from thirst when this happens. There may not be a drought where you are, but you can be still affected. Drought can kill crops. Then the price of food goes up for everyone.

9   In places like East Africa, droughts can be **devastating**. The drought there has caused thousands of people to die. In places with a lot of poverty, people cannot afford to pay higher food prices. So they eat less or go hungry. When this happens to many people at once, it is called a famine. Droughts are affecting crops around the world. So other countries have less to share to help people affected by famine.

10   Another place that is experiencing drought is the Amazon rainforest. The rainforests in Brazil are going through a "megadrought." That means that before they could recover from the last drought, another drought struck. The living things in the rainforest have **adapted** to a wet environment. They suffer when it is too dry. Many of the plants and animals are not found anyplace else. And this is bad news for us. Some of the plants in the Amazon are used to make important medicines.

11   So even if there is plenty of rain where you live, there are still a lot of reasons to be concerned. Your source of food may depend on rain in other parts of the country or the world. Many thousands of lives depend on rain. Plants and animals that don't live anyplace else depend on it. Conserving water is an important issue we should all care about!

Comprehension Check

1. Circle the letter next to the word that best describes how the author feels about droughts.

   a. hopeful

   b. angry

   c. worried

   d. sad

2. Circle the letter next to the reason that the author gives for thinking you might not care about droughts.

   a. You think food is too expensive.

   b. You do not live in an area with drought.

   c. You have never been to Africa.

   d. You think the rainforests have enough rain.

3. The author gives many reasons to care about droughts. With a partner, discuss which reasons you think are best at making you share his point of view. Why are these reasons so effective?

Because animal, Kids, and plants are dying

Independent Practice

Stop the Droughts! *continued*

RI.3.6

WORDS TO KNOW
continent
precious
wildfire

CITE EVIDENCE

A What does the author think is the worst thing about droughts? Put a star next to that sentence in paragraph 12.

B If there is the same amount of water in the world, why is the author worried? Underline the reason in paragraph 13. How does the author feel we should deal with droughts?

12 Drought is a problem that is happening around the world. Every **continent** is affected by it. In some places, people have to live with water restrictions. They can't water their lawns or wash their cars. In other places, food crops are dying because droughts are drying out the land. Droughts are causing famines and **wildfires**. The worst part is that scientists say droughts will happen more often.

13 The world has always had the same amount of water in it. The water we have evaporates into the sky and comes back down as rain. The water in your glass might be the same water that the dinosaurs drank. The problem is that the water isn't always where we need it. We need it in the places that people live and in places where food is grown. If some are wasting water, others may not have enough. So we have to be careful with our water supplies, conserve them, and keep them clean for ourselves and for all other living things on this planet. And because droughts are happening more often, we all need to pitch in and save our most **precious** resource.

14 By now, maybe you are serious about helping. Do you turn off the faucet while you brush your teeth? That could save gallons. Do you run tap water until it gets cold when you want a drink? That's a lot of clean water down the drain. Instead, fill a pitcher and put it in the refrigerator. Time yourself when you take a shower. The quicker you are, the more water you will save. But that's not all. We also need to use less energy to keep the planet from getting even hotter. Turn off the lights when you leave the room. Ride a bike. It's everyone's job to help the environment.

15 Remember, you can still be affected by a drought even if you live in an area with lots of rain. Remember also that by saving water at your home, you could be helping people who are experiencing drought somewhere else. Think of how amazing if would be if, through your actions, you could help people all over the world.

Comprehension Check

MORE ONLINE sadlierconnect.com

1. Circle the letter next to a problem caused by droughts.

    a. famine

    b. wildfires

    c. restrictions

    d. all of the above

2. Circle the letter next to the BEST summary of the author's point of view.

    a. We should help the victims of famine and send them food.

    b. We should turn off the water when we brush our teeth.

    c. We should care about droughts and help deal with them.

    d. We should learn more about the history of water.

3. What should people be doing about droughts, in this author's point of view? List as many of the author's specific recommendations as you can.

We should turn off the lights, turn off water and take shorter showers

Dust Bowl Disaster

(Genre: Personal Narrative)

1   My name is Jack Blanchard. I'm an elderly man now, but I'll never forget my childhood during the Dust Bowl. In 1925, my family moved to the Texas Panhandle. I was just 5 years old then. My parents dreamed of farming on their own land, so they bought a farmhouse with acres and acres of land. In a few years, they had transformed the land into great wheat fields. With the profits from the wheat, they were able to buy cows and chickens, too. We were real pioneers!

2   But the good times did not last long. By 1930, a severe drought turned the rich fields to sand and dust. The earth cracked and split open. Nothing would grow, not even weeds. Thick, choking dust covered everything.

3   Back then, I was just a young boy. I lived with my parents, grandpa, and five sisters. We were simple people who worked long hours, seven days a week. My sisters and I would wake up early before school to milk the cows or plow the fields. We took time off only to go to church on Sunday.

RI.3.4, RI.3.5, RI.3.6, RI.3.10

4   We took pride in our crops and animals. We weren't rich, but we had what we needed. Or we did until the drought came. The bone-dry conditions were constant and never let up. Those were the worst years of my life.

5   With the drought came fearful storms, nicknamed "dusters." The dust storms stung our eyes and itched our hair. It was hard to breathe. It got so bad that we had to cover our noses and mouths with wet cloths to block the dirt. To protect our eyes, we wore goggles to school.

6   The worst dusters were called "black blizzards." Those were scary because in the middle of the day, the world was dark. Night seemed to last all day.

7   It's hard to explain the impact of this disaster. During it, everyone and everything suffered. Farmers and ranchers couldn't work the land. The bodies of horses, cows, and pigs lay by the roads, filled with dirt. Jackrabbits invaded, eating everything in sight, and the birds flew far, far away. People got sick. Some died of lung disease from breathing in too much dust. Others died from not having food or water.

8   Filthy dust settled on buildings, automobiles, people, and animals. Sand piled up high outside homes. Sometimes we had to climb out of windows because it blocked doors. There was no escaping it. We used rags and tape to seal all the cracks in the windows and doors, but the dust still got in.

9   We had dust in our food and water. We ate dinner and ended up with grit in our teeth. My sisters and I could draw pictures in the dirt that lay on our dining table. Ma said there was no use hanging laundry out to dry. When we did, it looked dirtier than before it was cleaned!

Causes of the Dust Bowl

The Dust Bowl was set off by a very long drought and unusually high temperatures. Poor farming practices were used to increase profits. As a result, layers of grass that kept rich soil in place were seriously damaged. Topsoil dried out. Then high winds blew the soil. Dust clouds formed and turned into giant dust storms. Some of these storms were a mile high.

10   My teacher, Miss Evans, read us big-city newspaper accounts of what was going on. Our region in the middle of the country became known as the Dust Bowl. Many states, including Texas, Oklahoma, and Kansas, were affected. But the dusters were so powerful, people as far away as New York and Boston breathed in the dust, too. My grandpa said he felt like he was living in a desert. I said it looked like the moon.

11   We tried to stick it out, but it was clear we had to leave. We had survived three years of drought and dust storms. We said goodbye to our farm and friends, then we packed what we could fit in two old cars and left. The dust storms would continue for seven more years.

12   We headed west, just like millions of others, including folksinger Woody Guthrie. He also lived in Texas during that period and became famous as the "Dust Bowl Troubadour." He wrote and sang great songs about his experience in the Dust Bowl and about traveling west to California. His songs really captured what it was like to live through the great dust storms and then to pack up all you have and move west.

13   During our travels, no one knew what to expect from life out west. Unfortunately, life in California was hard, too. Jobs weren't always easy to find. The days were long and the pay was low. We lived in one-room shacks with no running water. But we escaped the dust, and at least we could breathe clean air.

14   My family was in California's Central Valley for 10 years. We picked lettuce, grapes, and oranges—whatever was in season. But we could never call California home. I was 23 and married, and I had two children when we returned to Texas. We rebuilt my parents' house and bought a new herd of cows. Now my children and grandchildren work the land.

15   This is Texas. It gets hot, and droughts still come and go. But in 2011, we had the driest year ever recorded. Some were calling it the New Dust Bowl. I just hope we learned a lesson from the Dust Bowl of my childhood. We must all do what we can to care for the earth.

To see more photos of the Dust Bowl, visit:
http://www.pbs.org/kenburns/dustbowl/photos/

Comprehension Check

1. Reread paragraph 11. Use context clues to choose the meaning of the word *stick* below. Circle the correct answer.

   a. to remain

   b. to poke

   c. to fasten

   d. a part of a tree

2. What information do you expect to find at the hyperlink on page 171?

   a. causes of the Dust Bowl

   b. Jack Blanchard's Dust Bowl memories

   c. images of the Dust Bowl

   d. the history of droughts

3. How does the text feature on page 170 help you understand "Dust Bowl Disaster"? Support your answer with text evidence.

It helps me understand Dust Bowl because it says drough and dust storms

4. Underline the last sentence of paragraph 4. Why does the author have this opinion? If you were the author, would you agree? Include details from the text to support your answer.

I would agree because I do not want to be in a Dust Bowl.

RI.3.9, SL.3.1.a, SL.3.1.c, SL.3.1.d, SL.3.4

Compare and Contrast Texts

In this unit, you read about hurricanes and tornadoes, floods, droughts, and an important event known as the Dust Bowl. Think about what you learned from these four texts. Then choose two of the texts and compare and contrast them using the Venn diagram below. List key details and important points from the texts to show the similarities and differences between them. Be prepared to discuss your ideas with your class.

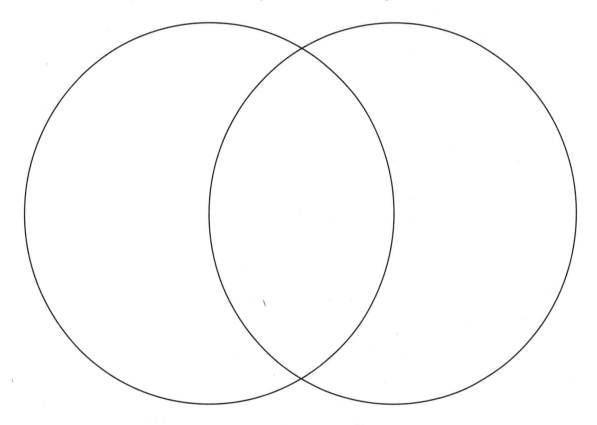

Return to the Essential Question

How can authors present informational text effectively?

In small groups or as a class, discuss the Essential Question. Think about what you have learned about word meanings, text features, and point of view. Use evidence from the four unit texts to answer the question.

L.3.4.b

Prefixes and Suffixes

Guided Instruction Prefixes and suffixes are word parts that are added to a base word to change its meaning. A prefix is added to the beginning of a base word. A suffix is added to the end of a base word. The new word's meaning is connected to the base word's meaning.

Read this sentence from "Dust Bowl Disaster": *The Dust Bowl was set off by a very long drought and unusually high temperatures.* In this sentence, the word *unusually* has a prefix in it. The prefix *un-* has been

added to the beginning of the base word *usually*. The word's meaning has changed from *usually* (or "normally") to *unusually* ("not usually").

The chart shows common prefixes and suffixes and their meaning.

Prefix	pre-	dis-	un-
Meaning	before	opposite of	not
Suffix	-er	-ful	-less
Meaning	one who	full of	without

Guided Practice Add a prefix or suffix from the chart to change the base word's meaning so that each sentence below makes sense.

1. When the lights go out, having candles is very use _ful_____.

2. Mia did not want to ___dis____ obey her parents.

3. The factory smoke made an ___un____ pleasant smell.

Independent Practice Each word below from "Dust Bowl Disaster" contains a prefix or a suffix. Write a separate sentence using each word.

powerful　　　　**rebuilt**

The stom was so powerful it knoked down many trees

The house had to be rebuilt after a hurrican

RI.3.4, RI.3.5, RI.3.6, L.3.4.b

Read the following passage in which vocabulary words, text features, and the author's point of view appear. Then answer the questions on pages 175 and 176.

Lightning Strikes!

(Genre: Magazine Article)

Stay Safe

1   Lightning kills more people than hurricanes or tornadoes. Only floods kill more people during storms. If a storm is near, stay inside. If you are outside during a storm, try to find shelter. If you can't get inside a building, stay away from tall trees and open fields. If you want to learn more about lightning, try **http://www.lightningsafety. noaa.gov/kids.htm.**

Zapped

2   No one knows how many people are hit by lightning each year. Even experts are unsure. Some say it's about 200, and others say it's more than 1,000. Although people can be killed by lightning strikes, most survive. People who were hit by lightning often have strange problems that doctors cannot explain. Their symptoms include headaches, forgetfulness, and trouble sleeping. A group of survivors meets every year in Tennessee to share stories. It's good to be around others who understand.

Fill in the circle of the correct answer choice.

1. What phrase in paragraph 1 is a clue to the meaning of *shelter*?

○ it is unsafe

○ during a storm

○ tall trees and open fields

◉ inside a building

2. Another word for *symptoms* in paragraph 2, line 5 is

○ explain

○ strange

◉ problems

○ strikes

RI.3.4, RI.3.5, RI.3.6, L.3.4.b

3. The word *strange* in paragraph 2 means

   ◉ not well understood

   ○ not very serious

   ○ cannot be cured

   ○ made-up or fake

4. In the last paragraph, *survivors* means

   ◉ people who lived

   ○ doctors who examine

   ○ lightning that strikes

   ○ groups that meet

5. Circle a subhead in the passage.

6. Underline the hyperlink in the passage.

7. What information do you expect to learn by using the hyperlink?

   How stay safe when lightning is around.

8. Put a box around the word with a prefix in paragraph 2, line 2. Give the prefix, the base word, and the word's meaning.

   Prefix = un   meaning
   base word = sure   not sure

9. What is the author's point of view about the meeting of lightning strike survivors? Use text evidence in your answer.

   The author's point of view is
   supportive because he thinks it's
   a good idea to be around others who understand

10. Do you agree with the author's point of view? Give reasons for your answer.

    I agree the author's point of
    view because I want to support
    those people

Introducing UNIT 8

I n this unit about extreme weather and pet safety, you will learn how to write an opinion piece. An opinion piece is sometimes called an argument.

When you write an opinion piece, you try to change the point of view of your readers or persuade them to do something. You might try to convince them to agree with your opinion on a school topic, a social problem, or a book.

To be effective, an opinion piece must be well organized and clearly written. Opinions should be supported by convincing reasons. Words should be chosen carefully, and the writing should follow grammatical rules.

Progress Check *Can I?*

Before Unit 8

After Unit 8

☐ State my opinion clearly. ☐

☐ Support my opinions with reasons. ☐

☐ Use linking words and phrases to connect my opinion and my reasons. ☐

☐ Include both an introduction and a conclusion. ☐

☐ Write using adjectives and adverbs correctly. ☐

☐ Write using correct spelling. ☐

☐ Write simple sentences. ☐

IN THIS UNIT, YOUR CHILD WILL...

- Learn to write an opinion piece with an introduction, a statement of opinion, reasons supporting it, and a conclusion.

- Learn to use linking words to connect the reasons to the opinion.

- Follow a process when writing an opinion piece, beginning with using an outline to organize ideas.

- Learn specific language skills to use when writing an opinion piece:

  - Use adjectives to describe nouns and adverbs to describe verbs.

  - Spell words using word families.

  - Write a variety of simple sentences.

NOTE: All of these learning goals for your child are based on the Grade 3 Common Core State Standards for English Language Arts.

I n this unit, children will learn about **writing to express an opinion.** Help your child see all the different types of opinion writing in the world around you, ranging from billboards and signs to movie reviews on websites and editorials in newspapers. Model responding to opinions by giving reasons that you agree or disagree with them.

When writing an opinion piece, it is important to pay attention to the **organization.** A good way for your child to organize his or her piece is to **list a reason to support an opinion,** and then **give details** to explain why that reason is important. Identify reasons and supporting information with your child in a published review or editorial. Decide together if the reasons and supporting details are convincing or not.

Activity: Focus on an important community issue. With your child, reach an opinion about it. Then together, write a letter to the editor of a local newspaper or contribute to a blog. In the first paragraph, introduce the topic and state your opinion. In the next paragraphs, give at least three reasons in support of your opinion. In the conclusion, restate your opinion and call for some sort of action. Then sign and submit!

WAYS TO HELP YOUR CHILD

Show respect for your child's opinions. Regularly engage in discussion with your child about topics he or she is passionate about, such as sports, hobbies, or movies. Ask for your child's point of view and follow up with questions requesting reasons: *Why do you say that? Do you know any facts that support your feelings?*

ONLINE

For more Home Connect activities, continue online at sadlierconnect.com

Text Types and Purposes: Write Opinion Pieces

Essential Question:
How do writers support their opinions?

W.3.1.a

CREATING AN ORGANIZATIONAL STRUCTURE

Ruthie used an outline to organize her essay. It has an opinion, three reasons to support this opinion, and a conclusion.

Title: _____

I. Introduction
    a. Background: _____
    b. Opinion: _____

II. Supporting Reasons
    a. Reason 1: _____
    b. Reason 2: _____
    c. Reason 3: _____

III. Conclusion
    _____

TITLE
- Draws the reader into the basic topic.

INTRODUCTION
- Introduces the topic.
- Gives background.
- States an opinion.

Underline the writer's opinion.

Read a Student Model

Ruthie is a student in Ms. Jenkin's third-grade class. Ruthie has been asked to write an opinion piece on what she would do with a pet during a natural disaster. In her piece, she must support her point of view with three reasons. As you read her essay, think about your opinion, reasons, and organization to prepare to write your own opinion piece.

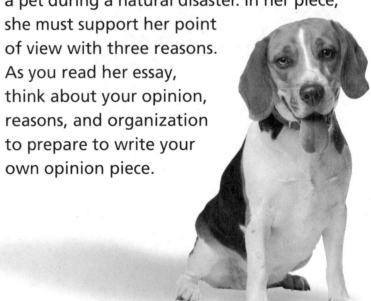

Any Pet in a Storm!

I know that there are a lot of natural disasters, such as hurricanes, tornadoes, and droughts, all over the world. The only one I can write about with real experience is a hurricane that hit my town last summer. When the hurricane hit, I was very worried about my beagle, Rudy, and what to do with him. My parents said we might have to leave our home without him. I think pet owners should always take their pets with them in a disaster.

W.3.1.b, W.3.1.c

First of all, our pets depend on us for everything—their food, their shelter, their health, and their happiness. These things don't change just because there is an emergency. We must take care of our pets no matter what! How would you feel if you were left alone in a scary emergency?

LINKING PHRASE
- Use linking words and phrases to link reasons to the opinion.

REASON 1
- Provide reasons that support the opinion.
- Ruthie uses *First of all* to link her reason and opinion.

Also, I know my dog, Rudy, is a part of the family. He comes on trips with us, eats dinner at the same time, and sits on the couch with me as I read. When I am sad, he always cheers me up, and I love him so much. Even thinking of leaving him behind in a hurricane gives me nightmares—imagining him hungry, scared, and alone.

REASON 2
Underline Ruthie's second reason.

Finally, it can be dangerous for other people when abandoned animals are trapped or roaming around. Imagine a rescue worker trying to search a house for survivors while a scared dog or cat tries to protect the house. The worker or the pet might get hurt. Also, if hungry animals roam the streets, they could get into trouble, like fighting each other and chasing or attacking people.

REASON 3
Underline Ruthie's third reason for never leaving pets behind.

Circle the linking word that connects this reason with Ruthie's opinion.

You should plan ahead for your pets in an emergency. Have a supply kit packed. Make sure your pet has its identification and shots, and plan to go to a safe place that allows pets if you have to leave your home. After you do all of this, you will never have to leave your pet behind in an emergency.

CONCLUSION:

- Ruthie's concluding statement wraps up her opinion essay and restates her opening opinion in slightly different words.

Underline Ruthie's concluding statement.

W.3.1.a–d, W.3.4, W.3.5, W.3.10

Use an outline like the one below to organize your opinion essay about something you care about. Then write a first draft of your essay on a separate sheet of paper. Remember to state an opinion and give three supporting reasons. Be sure to use linking words to connect ideas. You will use this draft to write your final essay in the Common Core Review section on page 190.

Title: _____

    I. Introduction

        a. Background: _____

        _____

        b. Opinion: _____

        _____

    II. Supporting Reasons

        a. Reason 1:_____

        _____

        _____

        b. Reason 2:_____

        _____

        _____

        c. Reason 3:_____

        _____

        _____

    III. Conclusion

        _____

        _____

L.3.1.a, L.3.1.g

Adjectives

Guided Instruction An **adjective** describes or tells about a noun. Adjectives often answer the questions "What kind?" or "How many?"

> The **strong** wind blew down many houses.

Sometimes adjectives are used to compare. To compare two nouns, add -*er* to the end of most adjectives.

To compare three or more nouns, add -*est* to the end of most adjectives.

> The puppy was **smaller** than the dog.
> The puppy was the **smallest** in the litter.

Guided Practice Underline the adjectives in each sentence.

1. The rain leaked through the old barn.

2. There were wet puddles everywhere.

3. The cold wind blew through the sides of the barn.

4. Several animals cuddled in the hay.

5. The nasty storm finally ended in the morning.

Independent Practice Circle the correct adjective in parentheses to complete each sentence.

1. The calf was the (younger, youngest) animal in the herd.

2. It was the (smaller, smallest) brother of the twins.

3. However, the calf was (smarter, smartest) than the bull.

4. It found the (drier, driest) hay of all in the barn.

5. After the storm, the calf was the (sleepier, sleepiest) animal in the barn.

L.3.1.a, L.3.1.g, L.3.6

Adverbs

Guided Instruction An **adverb** describes or tells about a verb. Adverbs often tell when, where, and how.

> *The wind blew **fiercely**.*
> ***Then,** the rain fell **everywhere**.*

Sometimes adverbs are used to compare. To compare two actions, add *-er* to the end of most one-syllable adverbs.

To compare three or more actions, add *–est* to the end of most one-syllable adverbs.

Guided Practice Underline the adverbs in each sentence.

1. Yesterday my cat was lost.

2. We looked outside for it.

3. After we won the baseball game, I ran happily all the way home.

4. My cat was on the front porch, meowing loudly.

Independent Practice Write the correct adverb in parentheses on the line.

1. The second lightning bolt flashed (quicker, quickest) than the first one.

   _____

2. That thunderclap was the (louder, loudest) I had ever heard.

   _____

3. The storm traveled (faster, fastest) than the one last week.

   _____

4. My little brother fell asleep (easier, easiest) than I did.

   _____

5. I was the one who slept the (sounder, soundest) in my family.

   _____

L.3.2.f, L.3.2.g, L.3.4.d

Correct Spelling

Guided Instruction When you are writing, it is important to spell the words you use correctly. Use what you know about other words to help you spell new words. You can use word families, syllable patterns, ending rules, and word parts such as suffixes and prefixes to help you spell words.

family   unfamiliar   familiarity   familiarize

You can use a dictionary to look up the correct spelling of words. You can also use a dictionary to look up the meaning of the word you are spelling, to make sure you are using the correct form of the word.

Guided Practice Write the base word that can help you spell the two words.

1. taken   mistake   _take_

2. retried   trying   _try_

3. caring   uncaring   _care_

4. interview   viewing   _view_

Independent Practice Write a word to complete each sentence, using a form of the base word in parentheses.

1. I was very ___excited___ to get a hamster. (excite)

2. I held it very ___carefully___ so I wouldn't harm it. (care)

3. Mom gave me little food ___dishes___ to put in its cage. (dish)

4. My hamster loves ___using___ its wheel to run around and around. (use)

5. I think my hamster's fur is ___beautiful___. (beauty)

L.3.1.i

Simple Sentences

Guided Instruction A **simple sentence** has one subject and one verb. It expresses one complete thought or idea.

- Simple: *The ground shakes during an earthquake.*

- Not Simple: *The ground shakes, and buildings move.*

Guided Practice Write *simple* or *not simple* to describe each sentence.

1. Yesterday there was an earthquake in our town. _simple_

2. I grabbed my dog, and we dashed under our table. _not simple_

3. My dog was shaking so I petted his fur and whispered soft words. _not simple_

4. None of our family was hurt in the earthquake. _simple_

5. We helped our neighbors, and the volunteers cleaned up the park. _not simple_

Independent Practice Write simple sentences.

1. _I see stars at night_

2. _I can drink milk_

3. _The kittens got adopted by the family_

4. _I feed my dog food_

5. _I can draw with my pencil_

SL.3.1.a–d, SL.3.3

Discuss the Essential Question

How do writers support their opinions?

Think about the Essential Question by responding to the questions below. Support your point of view with reasons and experience.

1. What words did the writer use to state her opinion?

_____

_____

2. What reasons did the writer state to support her opinion? How did the writer connect her reason to her opinion?

_____

_____

Use your notes above to discuss the Essential Question in small groups or as a class. Follow agreed-upon rules for discussion. Use the organizer below to record what you heard and how you participated.

Ideas I Agree or Disagree With		Questions I Asked
Agree		
Disagree		
New Ideas I Had During Discussion		**Questions I Answered**

L.3.1.a, L.3.1.g, L.3.1.i, L.3.2.f, L.3.2.g, L.3.4.d, L.3.6

This paragraph has mistakes in the use of adjectives and adverbs and in spelling. Write the paragraph correctly on the lines below. If you need help, look in a dictionary to check your spelling.

Last night a large storm came through. Dad and I spent the night in the barn careing for the animals. Each animal took cover. The chickens climbed to the higher point in the barn. The cows are our larger animals. Surprisingly, the pigs yelled the louder. The horses were very excitied and jittery. We put blankests on their backs. We tryed to keep them calm. Dad turned on the lights and played some soft music. It was a long night, but I am glad that I could help our animals.

_____

_____

_____

_____

_____

_____

_____

_____

_____

W.3.1.a–d, W.3.4, W.3.5, W.3.10

Assignment: Write an opinion essay about something you care about.

On the lines below, write the final copy of the opinion essay draft you created on page 183. It should start with an introduction and end with a conclusion. Be sure to include reasons that support your opinion. Make sure to use linking words to connect your reasons with your opinion. See the Writing Handbook (pages 275–283) for ways to improve your writing as you revise.

_____

_____

_____

_____

_____

_____

_____

_____

_____

_____

_____

_____

_____

_____

Introducing UNIT 9

Have you ever read two stories that were about the same characters? What kind of connections did you make about those characters when you read the second story? Maybe you remembered how they looked or what their personalities were like.

In the upcoming unit, the author has written four stories that involve the same two characters. In each story, the characters find themselves searching for answers in new situations. As you are reading, think about how the settings, events, and themes change with each story.

Pay close attention to the illustrations in each story, as well. What do the illustrations tell you about the stories? By the time you are done, you should be able to use these illustrations to find your own answers and make connections to the characters in the story!

Before Unit 9 ⬇ **Progress Check** *Can I?* **After Unit 9** ⬇

Before		After
☐	Explain how illustrations help you understand a story.	☐
☐	Compare and contrast the themes of stories with the same characters.	☐
☐	Compare and contrast the plots of stories with the same characters.	☐
☐	Compare and contrast the settings of stories with the same characters.	☐
☐	Use word roots as a clue to help find the meanings of words.	☐

HOME◆CONNECT...

IN THIS UNIT, YOUR CHILD WILL.

- Use illustrations to help better understand the meaning of the words in a story.

- Learn how to compare and contrast the settings, plots, and themes of texts featuring the same characters.

- Use a known word (for example, *medium*) to help define a lesser-known word with the same root (such as *medieval*).

- Compare and contrast three different texts featuring the same main characters: a mystery story and two adventure stories.

NOTE: All of these learning goals for your child are based on the Grade 3 Common Core State Standards for English Language Arts.

When students are able to combine what they read with what they see in **illustrations**, they are better able to understand the **characters, setting,** and **mood** of a text. As you are reading a story with illustrations, begin by having your child look at the illustrations and tell you what he or she is seeing. Then, read the text. Finally, ask your child about what he or she has seen and read and how the two go together.

Students enjoy reading a series of stories that feature the same characters. When characters are familiar, readers become interested in what will happen next in each story. In this unit, your child will read three stories featuring the same brother and sister duo. Being able to **compare and contrast** each one of these stories to the others is an important skill. As your child reads, ask him or her to pay attention to the details and themes in each story that are the same across texts and to look for ways in which each story is different.

WAYS TO HELP YOUR CHILD

The ability to compare and contrast situations, characters, and events is an extremely important skill. Help your child develop this skill by asking him or her leading questions, when appropriate. Read two different stories together, back-to-back, and ask your child to tell you how the stories are the same and how they are different. Have your child compare his or her two favorite movies or contrast one favorite sports team with another. Build the concept of comparing and contrasting into everyday conversations.

Activity: With your child, use descriptions in a text to create illustrations. First, do a web search on well-known illustrators, and look at some of the illustrations they have created. Then, read a favorite text-only story to your child, and work together to create illustrations to go along with the words.

ONLINE

For more Home Connect activities, continue online at sadlierconnect.com

Reading Literature: Integration of Knowledge and Ideas

Essential Question:
What connections can readers make?

Guided Instruction

RL.3.7

WORDS TO KNOW

cactus

expression

> **Illustrations** are pictures of the characters, setting, and events in a story.

CITE EVIDENCE

A **Illustrations** can help you picture a story's action. Look at the illustration below. In the story, underline the names of the **characters** in the illustration.

B The **setting** is where a story takes place. In the illustration, circle any pictures that tell you about the setting. Where does the story take place?

The Case of the Missing Fruit

(Genre: Mystery)

1   It was after lunch on Saturday, and Sofia and Tino were playing basketball. Their big sister, Ella, was home from college, and she was watching the children play while their parents were at work. Sofia was beating Tino by six points, and Tino was getting frustrated.

2   Sofia, on the other hand, was enjoying the game a little *too* much. "Hey, Tino, why did the chicken cross the road? To beat you at basketball!"

3   Tino started to get upset, and then he looked at Sofia's face. He had to laugh at her silly **expression**.

4   "Good one. But should you be clowning around when you are only winning by six points?"

5   "I don't know, hermano. Should I be?"

6   Before they could finish their game, a shout rang out from down the block.

7   "What was that?" Tino asked.

8   "I don't know," said Sofia, "but it sounded like it came from Mrs. Moreno's house."

9   Suddenly, another shout pierced the air. The two children and Ella ran toward the sound.

10   When the children arrived at Mrs. Moreno's, she was standing in her backyard, wearing thick gloves, and carrying a metal bucket.

11   "Mrs. Moreno," Ella asked, "are you all right?"

12   "Oh, *niños*, children, I didn't mean to frighten you."

13   "What happened?" asked Sofia.

14   "I came out to pick the fruit from my prickly pear **cactus** plants. It's time for me to make my prickly pear jam for the Labor Day picnic. When I got here, all of the cacti were bare!"

15   Tino and Sofia gave each other a look. They knew they had to help Mrs. Moreno.

16   "When was the last time you noticed the fruit?" Tino asked.

17   "I came outside this morning, and saw that the prickly pear fruit was ready to harvest. After that, I had to run some errands. Then, I came home, made an early lunch, and took a short nap."

18   "Has anyone asked about your prickly pears lately?" Sofia asked.

CITE EVIDENCE

C Illustrations let you see new characters in a story. Look at the picture of Mrs. Moreno. Then, box the words in the story that match the picture.

D Illustrations can help the reader visualize unfamiliar things in a story. Circle in the text what Mrs. Moreno is looking at. Have you seen a prickly pear cactus before?

Comprehension Check

Illustrations can show you the mood of the characters in a story. Look at the picture of Mrs. Moreno. What is her mood? How can you tell?

Guided Practice

The Case of the Missing Fruit *continued*

RL.3.7

WORDS TO KNOW
abnormal
investigate

CITE EVIDENCE

A Look carefully at the illustration. It shows one of the visitors Mrs. Moreno is describing in paragraph 19. Underline the sentences that match the illustration.

B Compare the illustration to the words in paragraph 19. What do you notice about the setting in the illustration that is not described in the story?

19 Mrs. Moreno answered Sofia, "Yesterday, Mr. Layton was walking his dog, and he stopped to tell me how good my plants were looking. This morning, Lisa Wu came over with some homemade bread from her mother. She made sure to tell me that she couldn't wait to try some jam soon. Then, Mr. Abbott from the pet store arrived. He told me he had never seen such vibrant red fruit!"

20 Tino could tell that Sofia's brain was working.

21 "I think we can find out what happened to the prickly pear fruit, but we need to **investigate**. Ella, would you mind driving us a few places?" she asked.

22 Ella answered, "Let's go solve a mystery!"

23 The first place they stopped was Lisa Wu's house. Lisa was in the front yard, watching her little brothers.

24 "Hey guys!" Lisa smiled at her visitors.

25 Tino spoke first. "We were wondering if you noticed anything **abnormal** at Mrs. Moreno's house this morning?"

26 Lisa thought for a minute. "Not that I can think of. Is something wrong?"

27 "All of the fruits from her prickly pear plants have been picked." Tino said.

28 "Oh no!" Lisa cried. "I have been looking forward to that jam all week!"

29 The next stop was Mr. Layton's house. No one was outside when Ella stopped, so the children rang the front doorbell. Mr. Layton came to the door.

30 "Hello, kids. How's it going?"

31   "Hi, Mr. Layton," Sofia said, "we have a question for you. When you were at Mrs. Moreno's house yesterday, did you notice anything strange?"

32   "Not at all," said Mr. Layton, "unless you count the fact that her prickly pear cactus plants always grow better than anything else in the neighborhood!"

Comprehension Check

1. Use the illustration to help you determine the meaning of the word *vibrant* in paragraph 19.

   a. sweet

   b. bright

   c. dark

   d. pale

2. Based on both the description of the setting in the story and the illustrations, where do you think this story takes place?

   a. in the mountains

   b. at the ocean

   c. in a forest

   d. in the desert

3. Work with a partner. Think about how you would draw an illustration of the characters and setting in paragraphs 29–32. What would your illustration look like?

   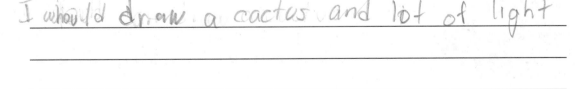
   I whould draw a cactus and lot of light

CONNECTING ILLUSTRATIONS AND TEXT

Independent Practice

RL.3.7

WORDS TO KNOW

evidence
healthy
review

CITE EVIDENCE

A Put a box around Sofia's dialogue that is connected to what she is saying in the illustration.

B Circle the item in the **illustration** that is related to Mr. Abbot's delivery.

The Case of the Missing Fruit *continued*

33   Sofia smiled, politely. "Thanks, Mr. Layton, that's all we needed to know."

34   The last stop was Mr. Abbott's pet store.

35   "Hey kids! What brings you this way?"

36   "We're helping out Mrs. Moreno," said Sofia. "You made a delivery to her house this morning. Can you tell us what it was?"

37   "Sure, I just dropped by to bring her some seed for her bird feeder."

38   Sofia smiled. "Did you just *deliver* the seed, Mr. Abbott, or did you also put it in the feeder?"

39   "Well, actually, I always fill her bird feeder for her as well."

40   "Thanks for your help, Mr. Abbott!"

41   Once the children were back in Ella's car, Sofia made an announcement. "I know who stole the prickly pear fruits! I'll tell you when we get to Mrs. Moreno's."

42   When they arrived, Mrs. Moreno was sitting on her front porch.

43   "Mrs. Moreno," Sofia said, "I think I know who stole your prickly pear fruit!"

44   "*Niña*, child, have you really solved the mystery? Who did this terrible thing?"

45   "First let's **review** the **evidence**: Mr. Layton noticed how **healthy** your cactus plants were looking. Lisa Wu's mom sent homemade bread, because she knew the fruits were ready to pick. And Mr. Abbott said how red the fruits were, as he filled your bird feeder."

RL.3.7

46   Before Sofia could finish, Tino gave a triumphant shout. "Of course! It wasn't a person who stole your cactus fruits, Mrs. Moreno. It was birds. The food Mr. Abbott put in your feeder attracted them to your yard, but they liked your beautiful red fruits even more. A perfect treat!"

47   Mrs. Moreno looked shocked, and then she began laughing. "I guess the case of the missing fruit has been solved!"

Comprehension Check   (MORE ONLINE) **sadlierconnect.com**

1. How would you describe the mood of the characters in the illustration on page 198?

   a. sad

   b. bored, uninterested

   c. excited, happy

   d. scared

2. Why is the filled bird feeder important to understanding how the fruit disappeared?

   a. It attracted birds to the cactus fruit nearby.

   b. It was not present when the cactus fruit disappeared.

   c. Mrs. Moreno did not want bird seed in her feeder.

   d. Mr. Abbott saw the cactus fruit when he filled the bird feeder.

3. If you paid close attention to the story and the illustrations, there were clues given to help you solve the mystery. What were those clues, both in the text and in the illustrations?

   The bird seeds and the bird feeder help to solve the mystery.

Guided Instruction

RL.3.9

WORDS TO KNOW

exploration
hammock
outskirts

Comparing two stories is looking at how they are the same. **Contrasting** two stories is looking at how they are different.

CITE EVIDENCE

A The first story took place in a neighborhood. Underline descriptions of the **setting** in this story.

B The first story featured many different **characters**. In this story, there are only four characters. Circle their names. What kind of adventure do you predict for the characters?

A Camping Adventure

(Genre: Adventure Story)

1   Tino finished rolling his sleeping bag and attached it to his backpack. "Hey, Sofia, I'm ready to go, " he called.

2   "Just give me one minute," his twin sister answered back.

3   Tino, Sofia, and their parents were leaving on an overnight camping trip in the Sonoran Desert, just outside of the city of Tucson, Arizona. They had come to Tucson for spring break. They had already visited many interesting places, including an old western movie set and a World War II airplane museum. Yesterday, the family decided that a camping trip would be the perfect way to end their week of fun and **exploration**.

4   Sofia grabbed her first-aid kit and shoved it into her backpack. "Last item! Let's go down to the hotel lobby and find Mamá and Papá!"

RL.3.9

(5)   They arrived at the Gilbert Ray campground right before lunch. They were given a campsite on the **outskirts** of the campground. They spent 30 minutes setting up camp: a large tent with three rooms, a fire pit, camp chairs, and a **hammock** stretched between two ironwood trees.

6   Sofia wanted to unroll their sleeping bags and get the cabin ready for the evening. Tino stopped her.

7   "What are you doing, sis?"

8   "I thought I would surprise everyone and make their beds for them for tonight."

9   "Well, they would get a surprise, all right."

10   "What do you mean?"

11   "Did you forget about scorpions?" answered Tino. "An unrolled sleeping bag is the perfect place for a scorpion to crawl in during the day. Imagine sliding into your sleeping bag tonight with one!"

12   "Ahh!" Sofia cried. "I can't believe I forgot that. Thanks for reminding me!"

13   "Any time, hermana!"

14   After lunch, Sofia, Tino, and their parents decided it was the perfect time for a nap. In the Sonoran Desert, it's best to sleep or relax during the heat of the day. Many of the animals do the same, in order to conserve their energy.

CITE EVIDENCE

C The first story was a **mystery** story, while this story is an **adventure** story. Box the paragraph that makes you think of an adventure story.

D In the first story, Sofia is in charge of solving the problem. Underline the name of the person who solves the problem in paragraph 11. Which problem is more serious?

Comprehension Check

Based on what you have read so far, how is this story the same as "The Mystery of the Missing Fruit"? How is it different?

COMPARING AND CONTRASTING STORIES

Guided Practice

RL.3.9

WORDS TO KNOW

endangered

environment

observation

CITE EVIDENCE

A Circle the animal that is featured among the setting in paragraphs 19 and 20. The first story also has an important animal. **Compare** the important animal from the setting of each story.

B Underline the plant that is featured in the setting in paragraph 18. How is it different from the plant in the first story?

A Camping Adventure *continued*

15   Once the temperature had dropped, Sofia asked her parents if they could all take a hike. "There are some desert plants I want to see, and I'm hoping to get a picture of some coyote tracks."

16   They decided to take one of the many small trails that intersected with their campground. The plan was to stop along the way to take pictures and explore the natural wonders of the desert.

17   Right away, Sofia noticed some interesting plants. "Take a look at these flowers, Papá. Can you look them up in your guidebook?"

18   Her father looked through his guidebook. "Wow, Sofia, that's a really rare plant. It's called the Kearney's Blue Star, and it's on the **endangered** species list. Make sure you get some good pictures, but don't touch it. We want to leave the **environment** just like we found it." Their father then reminded them of the old hikers' motto: *Take nothing but pictures, leave nothing but footprints.*

19   Tino was the next one to make a discovery. He stopped on the trail when he saw some animal tracks on the ground. "Look over here! Do you think these are coyote tracks?"

20   "Great powers of **observation**, Tino," said Papá. "Those are coyote tracks, for sure."

21   They hiked for a little while longer, and were just about to turn back for camp, when Tino spotted a small cave about ten feet off the trail.

22   "Mamá, Papá, can we go explore that cave?"

Comprehension Check

1. Choose the statement that best describes the settings of the first two stories.

   a. The first story mainly takes place in a pet store. This story mainly takes place in Tucson, Arizona.

   b. The first story mainly takes place in the desert. This story mainly takes place in a campground.

   c. The first story mainly takes place in a neighborhood. This story mainly takes place in the desert.

   d. The first story mainly takes place in Mrs. Moreno's yard. This story mainly takes place in Tino and Sofia's tent.

2. There are two new characters introduced in this story. Who are they?

   a. Abuela and Mr. Abbott

   b. Mamá and Papá

   c. Kearney's Blue Star and coyote

   d. Leo and Mr. Layton

3. Work with a partner. Name three ways that this story is different from the first story. Base your answer on details from both stories.

_____

_____

_____

COMPARING AND CONTRASTING STORIES

RL.3.9

WORDS TO KNOW
admiring
vein
wildlife

CITE EVIDENCE

A The plots of this story and the last story both focus on nature. Circle the narrator's description of a natural event.

B In paragraph 33, underline the sentences that describe a **theme**, or main idea, of this story. What was the main idea of the first story?

A Camping Adventure *continued*

23 Papá considered for a moment. "The cave doesn't look big enough for any **wildlife**, so it's probably safe. But, I would like to check it out first."

24 They hiked over to the cave, and Papá looked inside with his flashlight. It wasn't what he expected. The cave was a large room, big enough for people to stand up. Papá went in first, and the family followed.

25 Papá moved his flashlight around the walls. Suddenly, Sofia gasped. "Papá, shine the flashlight back in that corner."

26 As he moved his light to the back of the room, Tino said, "Wow!" while Mama caught her breath. Papa just looked on in wonder.

27 At the back of the cave was one of the most beautiful rock walls any of them had ever seen. It was covered in sparkling shades of green, blue, and red. A small stream of water curled down the wall, highlighting a colored path as it flowed.

28 "What is it, Papá?" Sofia asked.

29 "I'm not completely certain," her father said, "but I think we may have discovered a rare copper **vein.** When the chemicals in the water mix with the chemicals in the rock, it creates colors on the wall."

30 The family members stood quietly, **admiring** the beauty of the cave. After a few minutes, Mamá reminded them that it was time to leave.

31 "This is spectacular," she said quietly, "but we do need to get back to camp before dark."

32   As they left the cave to head back into the desert, Tino turned to his sister. "I don't know about you, Sofia, but I feel like we saved the best part of our spring break trip for last."

33   Sofia smiled. "I'm with you, *hermano*. That was the most amazing thing I have ever seen. What a cool adventure!"

Comprehension Check   MORE ONLINE   sadlierconnect.com

1. Based on your understanding of the setting, what is the meaning of the phrase "copper vein" in paragraph 29?

   a. a streak of copper in the rock wall

   b. the way chemicals react

   c. how blood flows through the body

   d. a copper picture in the cave

2. Based on both stories, which character would you describe as intelligent, with a love for the outdoors?

   a. Papá

   b. Sofia

   c. Mrs. Moreno

   d. Mr. Layton

3. Compare and contrast the themes of the first two stories. How are the themes the same? How are they different? Cite text evidence.

_____

_____

_____

_____

_____

Treasure in the Desert

(Genre: Adventure Story)

1   It was 3:05 on Friday, and Sofia Rivera was searching for her twin brother, Tino. School was already over, and it wasn't like Tino to hang around. They were staying with their *abuela*, or grandmother, for the weekend, and she would be waiting. Sofia decided to check the school library. She found Tino putting an old, dusty book in his backpack.

2   "Tino, hurry! Abuela will be waiting outside."

3   "Okay, Sofia, but wait until you see the book I just found!"

4   That evening, after they said goodnight to their grandmother, Tino came into Sofia's room. "We need to talk," he said.

5   "Does this have anything to do with that book you checked out from the library?"

6   "It does. It's a book about finding gold and jewels in Arizona's deserts. I thought it would make an interesting book report. But, as I was reading, I noticed something curious."

7   Tino opened the book and slowly turned the pages in the last chapter. "Look at the bottom of the pages," he said.

8   "It looks like someone has drawn a map in the book," Sofia said. "Do you know what it leads to?"

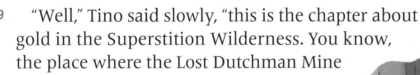

9   "Well," Tino said slowly, "this is the chapter about gold in the Superstition Wilderness. You know, the place where the Lost Dutchman Mine is located?"

10   "Do you think this map could help us find the most famous lost treasure in Arizona?"

11   "Maybe!" Tino winked at his twin sister.

RL.3.7, RL.3.9, RL.3.10

12   Saturday dawned clear and sunny. Tino and Sofia got up early and cooked breakfast for their abuela.

13   Tino explained to his grandmother about the dusty old book from the library, and how he believed it held a map to the Lost Dutchman Mine.

14   "And you want us to follow the map, to see if we can locate the lost treasure?" Abuela asked.

15   "It would be a fun adventure," Sofia said.

16   Abuela considered for a moment. "Okay!" she said at last. "Let's go find a treasure!"

17   Hiking in the desert requires special precautions. They packed water, trail mix, and sunblock. They wore long pants, protective hats, and hiking boots. At the Superstition Wilderness area, Tino pulled out his map and compass.

18   "We need to take the trail into the Superstition Wilderness for about 300 yards, then veer off to the north."

19   They grabbed their packs and checked in at the ranger station. Then they followed the trail into the desert.

20   Suddenly, Tino stopped. "Look at that saguaro cactus!"

21   In front of the group was a giant saguaro cactus with a peculiar shape. It had four arms that pointed straight down.

22   "Now," Tino said, "look at the map."

23   Sure enough, there was a drawing of a cactus with four arms pointing down.

24   "We're on the right trail!" Tino exclaimed. "Next, we need to turn west until we see a rock shaped like a castle."

25   Abuela was the one who spotted it first. "Children, *niños*, look. Does that giant rock look like a castle to you?"

26   Tino studied his map. "Behind the rock, there should be a small opening. That's where we need to dig!"

27   They started digging, taking turns to avoid overheating. Eventually, Sofia spoke up, "I think I've found something!"

28   She uncovered a small leather pouch.

29   "Whoa," Tino breathed, "I bet this is it. It's probably some old money that's worth millions of dollars today."

30   "Why don't you open it and see?" Abuela chimed in.

31   Tino opened the leather pouch. He carefully pulled out a thin yellow sheet of paper. There was old-fashioned writing.

32   "My name is Josef Walzer," he read. "People around here call me 'The Dutchman,' but I am actually a German immigrant. I came to America to make my fortune. I was driven by a desire for gold.

33   "I spent years searching for gold, but never found anything. I returned to civilization, but I had no money and no place to live. A kind old woman who owned a small restaurant agreed to take me in, if I would work for her. She let me cook for the restaurant, and that's when I found my real treasure—I was a talented chef.

34 "I created a recipe for Dutch Apple Pie that everyone loved. Customers came from miles around to try my Lost Dutchman Pie. Now I have no one to leave the secret of my famous pie to. I am burying the recipe in the desert. I've left a map in my old guidebook. Hopefully, someone worthy will find my valuable treasure."

35 Tino turned the letter over. Sure enough, on the back, was a recipe for Lost Dutchman Pie.

36 Tino, Sofia, and Abuela looked at each other, not sure what to say. Suddenly, Sofia burst out laughing. "It's not the Lost Dutchman Mine; it's the Lost Dutchman Pie!"

37 Tino and Abuela joined in with her laughter. "Tino," Abuela said, "thank you for this adventure."

38 "But we didn't find any gold," Tino said.

39 "Maybe not, " Abuela answered back, "but we did find a treasure. I don't know about you, but I can't wait to uncover the mysteries of the Lost Dutchman Pie. Dessert, anyone?"

Comprehension Check

1. Compare and contrast this story to "A Camping Adventure." Which new character is introduced in this story?

   a. Mamá

   b. Leo

   c. Abuela

   d. Mrs. Johnson

2. Based on the text and illustrations, which statement best describes the setting of this story?

   a. a neighborhood

   b. a classroom

   c. the high desert

   d. an old movie set

3. Think about the illustrations in this story. How do the illustrations help you learn more about the characters and the setting in this story? Use examples from the story in your answer.

The pictures helped me see and understand what the setting looks like and character

4. This story and the second story, "A Camping Adventure," are both adventure stories. But, they have very different themes. Compare and contrast the themes of these two stories.

The first one was a adventure one and the other one is a mystery.

RL.3.9, SL.3.1.a, SL.3.1.c, SL.3.1.d, SL.3.4

Compare and Contrast Texts

In this unit, you read stories that featured the same characters in different situations. Think about how these stories are the same, and how they are different. Then choose two of the texts and compare and contrast them using the T-chart below. List important details about setting, characters, and theme to show how the texts are similar or different. Be prepared to discuss your ideas with the class.

Similarities	Differences
• both desserts • Tino • Sofia	• camping • cave • mystery and adventure

Return to the Essential Question

What connections can readers make?

In small groups or as a class, discuss the Essential Question. Think about what you have learned about making connections between illustrations and texts, and about how you can compare and contrast setting, theme, and characters in different stories. Use evidence from the three unit texts to answer the question.

L.3.4.c

Roots

Guided Instruction Looking at the **root** of a word and comparing it to a familiar word with the same root can help you understand a word's meaning.

Root	port	cause or cus	vent	vac
Meaning	carry	reason	come	empty

Root	civ	fac	migra	vert
Meaning	citizen	do, make	wander	turn

Guided Practice Identify the root of each word below.

1. fact: _____ face _____

2. immigrant: _____ migrat _____

3. report: _____ port _____

Independent Practice Identify the root, and its meaning, in each of the words in **bold** below. Then in the sentence that follows, use what you have learned to write the meaning of the bold word with the same root. Use a dictionary if necessary.

1. "Tino," Abuela said, "thank you for this **adventure**."
   Root/meaning: _____ vent _____
   The people at the comic book **convention** came from all over the world.
   Word meaning: _____ vent _____

2. "I gave up and moved back to **civilization**."
   Root/meaning: _____ civ _____
   The volunteers who cleaned up the park were very **civic** minded.
   Word meaning: _____ civ _____

RL.3.7, RL.3.9, L.3.4.c

Read the following mystery story. Think about how this story is the same as the previous stories in this unit and how it is different. Then answer the questions on pages 213 and 214.

The Missing Pencil Sharpener
(Genre: Mystery)

1   Sofia and Tino were in their home classroom. Ms. Johnson, their teacher, stood in front of the class with two students.

2   "Class, I have a mystery. When I got to school, my classroom was vacant, and my pencil sharpener had disappeared. Can you discover which one of these two students took it?"

3   Sofia raised her hand and asked one of the students, "Where were you when the sharpener was taken?" The boy smiled and said, "I was outside."

4   Tino quizzed the other student. "Where were you when the sharpener was taken?" "I was in the cafeteria," she said.

5   Sofia closely inspected the students and then said, "The boy did it. His excuse is not true. It's raining, and his shoes are clean. If he'd been outside, they would be muddy and wet!"

6   Ms. Johnson laughed, "I should have known you two would win my mystery challenge!"

Fill in the circle of the correct answer choice.

1. What is the setting of this story?

○ the desert
○ a neighborhood
◉ a classroom
○ the pet store

2. What new character appears in paragraph 1?

◉ Ms. Johnson
○ Mr. Abbott
○ Abuela
○ April

3. Which story in this unit has a theme most like "The Missing Pencil Sharpener"?

   ○ "A Camping Adventure"

   ○ "Treasure in the Desert"

   ◉ "The Case of the Missing Fruit"

4. Which characters appear in all of the stories in this unit?

   ○ Sofia and Abuela

   ◉ Tino and Sofia

   ○ Mamá and Papá

   ○ Ella and April

5. Identify the root of the word *excuse* in paragraph 5.

   The root cuse

6. Name this story's genre. Name another unit story in this genre.

   This story's gene is mystery

7. Who announces the solution to the mystery in both stories?

   Sofia in both stories

8. Compare the character of Ms. Johnson in "The Missing Pencil Sharpener" to Mrs. Moreno in "The Case of the Missing Fruit."

   Mrs. Moreno was missing her fruit. Both missing

9. What would a picture of this story's setting look like?

   Classroom

10. How would you illustrate "The Missing Pencil Sharpener"?

    I will put a picture

Introducing UNIT 10

In this unit about the desert, you will learn how to research and write a report. The purpose of a research report is to provide information.

When you write an informative text, such as a research report, you will begin by gathering information on your topic. You will want to find several different sources for information, and then organize this information into related ideas. You will introduce the topic in the beginning, and end with a statement or paragraph that tells what the reader just learned. Linking words such as *also*, *another*, and *but* can help you show how ideas are related.

To be effective, a research report should use facts, definitions, and details to explain the ideas and develop the topic.

Progress Check *Can I?*

Before Unit 10		After Unit 10
☐	Conduct a research project.	☐
☐	Gather and take notes on information from print and digital sources.	☐
☐	Group related information together.	☐
☐	Provide information that builds knowledge about a topic.	☐
☐	Write using compound sentences correctly.	☐
☐	Write using complex sentences correctly.	☐
☐	Capitalize the important words in a title.	☐

HOME✦CONNECT...

- Learn to write a research report that builds knowledge about a subject.

- Gather information by taking notes from print and digital sources.

- Group related information in a report.

- Learn specific language skills and use them in writing a research report:

  - Write compound and complex sentences, using conjunctions correctly.

  - Capitalize the important words in a title.

NOTE: All of these learning goals for your child are based on the Grade 3 Common Core State Standards for English Language Arts.

I n this unit, children will learn about writing a **research report** to share knowledge about a topic. Discuss with your child a topic that you know about, such as repairing a car or baking bread. Share how you continue to learn more. For example, you may read books, talk to other people, or do research on the Internet. Point out that there are a great many resources that can give you the information you need.

Your child will begin the process by **researching a topic**. He or she will use **research materials,** such as books and websites. To practice researching on the Internet, discuss a topic and help your child find good sources of Internet information on it. (Sites ending in .edu and .gov are the most reliable.) As you read information on the topic together, **write down facts and details** that are related. Help your child understand that **related information is grouped together** in a research report.

WAYS TO HELP YOUR CHILD

Encourage your child to write often and for a variety of purposes. For example, your child can write thank-you notes and letters to family and friends, a journal entry on a scrap-book page, or a list of instructions for taking care of a pet. As your child writes, discuss the purpose for that kind of writing and how it is unique.

Conversation Starter: A research report is an opportunity to build knowledge on a topic by searching for answers. Discuss these questions with your child: *What is an expert? How does someone become an expert? What are you an expert at? On what topic would you like to become an expert? How might you learn more about that topic?* Emphasize that writing is a great way to learn from and share knowledge with others.

ONLINE

For more Home Connect activities, continue online at sadlierconnect.com

Research to Build and Present Knowledge: Write Research Reports

Essential Question:
How do writers conduct and present research on a topic?

W.3.7, W.3.8

CREATING AN ORGANIZATIONAL STRUCTURE

Bharat used an outline to organize his report. It is divided into three sections: introduction, explanation, and conclusion.

```
I. Introduction
   Topic:
   _____

II. Explanation
   a. Subtopic 1:
   _____
   _____

   b. Subtopic 2:
   _____
   _____

III. Conclusion
   _____
   _____
```

INTRODUCTION

- Bharat introduces the topic at the beginning, leading up to a statement about what the report will be about.

Underline the sentence that tells what Bharat's report will be about.

Read a Student Model

Bharat has been asked to write a research report about the desert. He has researched sources, taken notes, and then grouped related information together. As you read Bharat's research report, think about how you might research your own report about the desert and how you might use the facts, definitions, and details you find to build readers' knowledge.

Life in the Desert

What do you think of when you imagine a desert? Many people think of sand, rocks, or cacti. They might be surprised to know that the desert is home to many different animals, from snakes to birds to rabbits. The desert presents many challenges to animals. They must be able to survive the strong heat and the limited rainfall. However, many animals are uniquely suited to living in these harsh conditions. Let's take a look at some animals that make their home in and around the saguaro cactus.

W.3.7, W.3.8

Inside the Cactus

The saguaro cactus has long arms that reach toward the sky. They are covered with a tough coating and spikes. The spikes help to keep water in and animals out. Yet, some animals make their way through these barriers and nest inside the soft flesh of the cactus. For example, the woodpecker uses its beak to peck holes in the trunk and branches. It hollows out the soft inside to make a nest. Later, when the woodpecker leaves, elf owls, purple martins, and sparrows may use the abandoned nest for their home.

Under the Cactus

Under the saguaro cactus stretches the sandy desert floor. Many animals may be found scurrying across the dry landscape in search of food and water. Several animals eat the cactus's flesh. They include such animals as pack rats, jackrabbits, mule deer, and bighorn sheep. In the late summer, the cactus bears fruit. This fruit is a source of energy for several animals. The saguaro cactus has thick channels inside that hold water for the plant. This channel is a source of water for animals when needed.

ORGANIZATION

- Bharat has gathered information about desert life from different sources. Some sources are printed materials. Other sources are digital or online.
- He has grouped related information together, using headings to show each grouping.

Circle two details about different animals that use the inside of the saguaro cactus.

DEVELOP THE TOPIC

- Facts and other details that Bharat has researched help build readers' knowledge about the topic.

Underline two facts in the section "Under the Cactus."

CONCLUDING STATEMENT

- Bharat's ending wraps up the report by summing up what the reader has learned.

Underline the sentence that is the concluding statement.

The desert can be a harsh place to live. The animals living there face many challenges. Despite this, many animals make their homes in the desert. They depend on the natural resources such as the saguaro cactus to survive. So, the next time you think of the desert, you may think of rocks, sand, and cacti. However, you also should think about woodpeckers, hawks, jackrabbits, mule deer, and bighorn sheep. The desert is home to a surprising number of animals.

Sources:

http://www.saguaro.national-park.com/info.htm#Life
http://www.nps.gov/sagu/planyourvisit/upload/The%20Saguaro%20Cactus.pdf
"Saguaro," Encyclopædia Britannica

W.3.7, W.3.8

Use a graphic organizer like the one below to take notes for your research report on the desert. You may use print or digital sources to find information. You will use these notes to create your outline on page 222.

Source 1	Source 2
Summarize or paraphrase information: lots of spikes to keep the water in and the animals stay out. The cactus is also a source for animals.	Summarize or paraphrase information: There are a lot of plants and animals living in the desert.

WRITE RESEARCH REPORTS

W.3.4, W.3.5, W.3.7, W.3.8, W.3.10

Use an outline like the one below to organize your research report about the desert. Then write a first draft of your report on a separate sheet of paper. Be sure to take good notes and group related information together. You will use this draft to write your final research report in the Common Core Review section on page 228.

I. Introduction

Topic:

_____

_____

II. Explanation

a. Subtopic 1:

_____

_____

_____

_____

b. Subtopic 2:

_____

_____

_____

_____

III. Conclusion

_____

_____

_____

_____

Compound Sentences

Guided Instruction A **compound sentence** combines two simple sentences that have related ideas. A connecting word called a **conjunction** (*and, but, or*) joins the two sentences. Always use a comma before the conjunction in a compound sentence.

Read these related sentences.

Some desert plants have needles. Not all plants have them.

To write these two sentences as a compound sentence, use a conjunction.

Some desert plants have needles, but not all plants have them.

Guided Practice Complete each sentence using a conjunction (*and, but, or*).

1. We will camp in the desert, _____and_____ we will go to the beach.

2. I like camping in the desert, _____but_____ it can get cold at night.

Make each pair of sentences into a compound sentence.

3. Be sure to bring sunscreen. You might get a sunburn.

   Be sure to bring sunscreen, or you might get sunburn.

4. You should wear hiking boots. You might want a hat.

   You should wear hiking boots, and you might want a hat.

Independent Practice Write two of your own compound sentences. Use a different conjunction in each sentence. Be sure to use a comma before the conjunction.

1. I will go hiking, but I have to go with my parents.

2. You might want to bring sneakers, or you can bring a pair of flip-flops.

L.3.1.h, L.3.1.i

Complex Sentences

Guided Instruction A **complex sentence** is made up of two related ideas joined together by a subordinating conjunction. Some common **subordinating conjunctions** are *after*, *as if*, *because*, *before*, *since*, *though*, and *when.*

Read these related sentences.

We filled our water bottles. We went on a hike.

To write these two sentences as one complex sentence, use a subordinating conjunction.

*We filled our water bottles **before** we went on a hike.*

Guided Practice Complete each of these complex sentences. Use the subordinating conjunction *until* or *because*.

1. We will walk on the path ____until____ we get to the ranger station.

2. ____Because____ we had hiked for so long, I was really tired.

Make each pair of sentences into a complex sentence using a subordinating conjunction.

3. Beth led our hike. She had the map.

____Beth led our hike because she had the map.____

4. We were lost. We used our compass.

____We were lost before we used our compass.____

Independent Practice Write two of your own complex sentences using a subordinating conjunction.

1. ____After we go to school, we will meet up at the park.____

2. ____Since it was the last day of school, we all watched a movie (Because of Winn-Dixie).____

Capitalization

Guided Instruction A title tells the name of a book. The first word and all the important words are capitalized. Words such as *a*, *an*, *and*, *but*, *for*, *in*, *of*, *or*, *the*, and *to* are not capitalized unless they are the first word.

A Guide to Deserts
Camping in the Desert

Guided Practice Circle the letters that should be capitalized in each title.

1. ants and other desert insects
2. a bird lover's look at deserts
3. looking for snakes
4. the hidden life of desert animals

Independent Practice Write each book title correctly.

1. *look at the sand and rocks*

   Look at the Sand and Rocks

2. *lizard's big adventure*

   Lizard's Big Adventure

3. *ollie owl flies at night*

   Ollie Owl Flies at Night

4. *what's under the rock?*

   What's Under the Rock?

5. *a really hot day and a cold night*

   A Really Hot Day and a Cold Night

SL.3.1.a–d, SL.3.3

Discuss the Essential Question

How do writers conduct and present research on a topic?

Think about the Essential Question by responding to the questions below. Support your point of view with reasons and experience.

1. What topic did the writer develop into a research report?

_____

_____

2. How did the writer group related information together?

_____

_____

_____

Use your notes above to discuss the Essential Question in small groups or as a class. Follow agreed-upon rules of discussion. Use the organizer below to record what you heard and how you participated.

Ideas I Agree or Disagree With		Questions I Asked
Agree		
Disagree		
New Ideas I Had During Discussion		**Questions I Answered**

L.3.1.h, L.3.1.i, L.3.2.a

This paragraph has mistakes in compound and complex sentences and in capitalization. Write the paragraph correctly on the lines below.

> We read the book the deserts of texas in class. The book had many interesting facts it showed lots of beautiful pictures. This book was helpful, because we are writing desert reports. Today, our teacher showed us pictures of desert flowers. I was surprised at how many there are. Tomorrow, we will read a book called I live in the desert. The book tells about different desert animals. After that, we will share what we learned. We may create a poster about desert animals or we may write a report about them.

We read the book The Deserts of Texas in class. The book had many intreresting facts, and it showed lots of beautiful pictures. This book was helpful because we are writing desert reports, and today our teacher showed us pictures of desert flowers. I was suprised at how many there are, but tomorrow, we will read a book called I Live in the Desert. The book tells about different desert animals, and after that, we will share what we learned. We may create a poster about desert animals, or we may write a report about them.

W.3.4, W.3.5, W.3.7, W.3.8, W.3.10

Assignment: Research and write a report about a desert topic.

On the lines below, write your final copy of the research report draft you created on page 222. Be sure to group related evidence together. As you write, use the evidence you have found to build knowledge about the topic. Remember to list your sources at the end of the report. See the Writing Handbook (pages 275–283) for ways to improve your writing as you revise.

_____

_____

_____

_____

_____

_____

_____

_____

_____

_____

_____

_____

_____

_____

_____

Introducing UNIT 11

What do you see when you look into the sky at night? How much do you know about our solar system? In this unit, you will learn more about the solar system and the ways we study it.

This unit focuses on science topics. It includes a how-to manual, a magazine article, an editorial, and an explanatory text. These are all informational texts. Each one provides the reader with facts about a topic. Authors who write informational texts organize their writing clearly. They also present interesting details. Informational texts usually include photos, graphs, and charts. These images may include additional information that is not stated in the text.

You can learn a lot from an informational text. You also can learn a lot from comparing texts on the same topic. Let's see what you discover as you read this unit!

Progress Check *Can I?*

Before Unit 11

After Unit 11

- [ ] Connect photos and other visual information to an informational text. [ ]

- [ ] Understand the structure, such as causes and effects and sequence of events, of an informational text. [ ]

- [ ] Compare and contrast important information in two informational texts. [ ]

- [ ] Understand differences of meaning among related words. [ ]

HOME ◆ CONNECT...

It is important for readers to learn how to connect **visual information** (such as photographs, illustrations, graphs, and charts) **and text** to understand what they read. Find a magazine article that includes a number of images. Share it with your child, and discuss how the images add to the text.

Cause and effect is a type of **text structure** that nonfiction authors use to organize their writing. Talk with your child about a recent news event. Discuss the reasons why it happened and what occurred (the cause and effect). Work together with your child to create a two-column chart that lists causes and effects related to the event.

This unit includes a magazine article and an editorial about the same topic: the dwarf planet Pluto. It can be helpful to **compare and contrast texts** about the same subject to better understand a topic. Find a newspaper story and a newspaper editorial on the same subject. Share the two articles with your child. Discuss how they are alike and how they are different.

Activity: Work together with your child to search for articles about the universe and space exploration on the Internet. Narrow the topic as you choose links to explore. Use correct terms for the images you see on screen, such as *photograph, illustration, graph,* etc. Discuss why some of the articles are easier to follow or more appealing than others. List interesting facts, and create your own fact sheet about space.

IN THIS UNIT, YOUR CHILD WILL..

- Connect photographs, illustrations, and other examples of visual information to text.

- Describe text structure—how information and ideas are related—in an informational text.

- Identify causes and effects and sequences of events in a text.

- Compare and contrast the most important points in two texts on the same topic.

- Understand different meanings among related words.

- Compare and contrast four texts on the same theme: a technical text, a magazine article, an editorial, and a scientific text.

NOTE: All of these learning goals for your child are based on the Grade 3 Common Core State Standards for English Language Arts.

WAYS TO HELP YOUR CHILD

Demonstrate a positive attitude toward reading and learning. Find articles to read with your child. Before you read, pose questions about the topic. You should ask questions you hope the article will address. Encourage your child to ask questions, too. Create a list that includes your questions and those of your child. Then as you read through the article together, search for the answers.

> **ONLINE**
> **For more Home Connect activities, continue online at** sadlierconnect.com

Reading Informational Text: Integration of Knowledge and Ideas

Essential Question:
How can authors use text structure to connect ideas and information?

RI.3.7

WORDS TO KNOW

astronomer
reflecting telescope
refracting telescope
solar system

Informational text often includes photos, charts, diagrams, or other kinds of **visual information**. These images help support the text.

CITE EVIDENCE

A Technical text provides information through **images** and written information. Circle the paragraph that describes the image on this page.

B Place a box around the paragraph that describes a telescope that is not shown as an image.

How to Make a Telescope

(Genre: Technical Text)

1   Hello, budding **astronomers**! Do you want to study objects in the **solar system**? This manual provides all the information you need to build your own telescope. When you are done, you will be able to see the stars and the planets. You might even spot a comet or two!

2   Before you begin, it is important to know how telescopes work. A telescope is a tool that makes distant objects look close.

3   This manual explains how to build a **refracting telescope**, which is made with lenses. You will use two magnifying glasses as your lenses. A refracting telescope shows objects upside down.

4   A refracting telescope is different from a **reflecting telescope**, which is made with mirrors. The world's first telescopes were the refracting kind. Today, most telescopes are the reflecting kind. These are more complicated and harder to build on your own.

5   Follow these instructions to put your refracting telescope together. First, make sure you have everything you will need.

Refracting Telescope

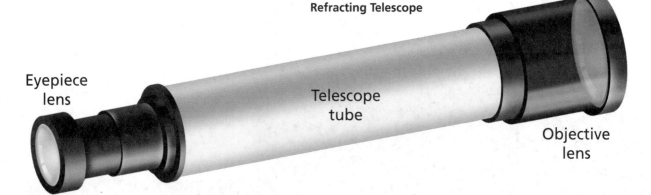

Eyepiece lens

Telescope tube

Objective lens

RI.3.7

6   Gather the following items:

  • Two magnifying glasses, one big and one small
  • A long cardboard tube
  • A roll of masking tape
  • A black marker
  • A piece of newspaper
  • A pair of scissors
  • Measuring tape
  • A friend to lend a hand

7   Now, assemble your telescope.

8   **Step 1:** First, take the newspaper and place it on a table or other flat surface. Hold the big magnifying glass over the paper so the printing appears blurry, or hard to read.

9   **Step 2:** Take the small magnifying glass into your other hand. Hold it between your eyes and the big magnifying glass. Move the small magnifying glass forward and back. Stop when you see the newspaper come into focus in the large magnifying glass. The printing will appear both larger and upside down.

Comprehension Check

How does the list on this page relate to the image on the page? Include evidence from the text in your answer.

CITE EVIDENCE

C The **illustrations** in a text connect to the words, helping the reader to see key details. Draw a box around the lenses in the text and in the Figure A image.

D Illustrations can also help by showing the reader the steps in a process. Circle the text that tells you in what order the telescope assembly occurs. How does seeing the items help you understand the circled text?

Figure A

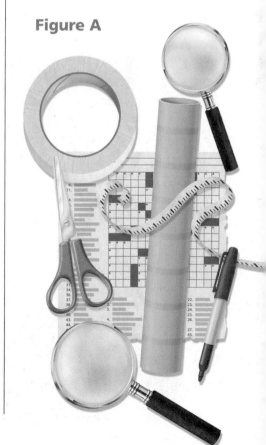

Guided Practice

How to Make a Telescope *continued*

RI.3.7

WORDS TO KNOW
centimeter
excess

CITE EVIDENCE

A Circle the step that explains how to cut a slot into the tube and what the slot is for.

B Draw a box around the letter of the figure that illustrates Step 4. In your own words, what does that illustration show?

Figure C

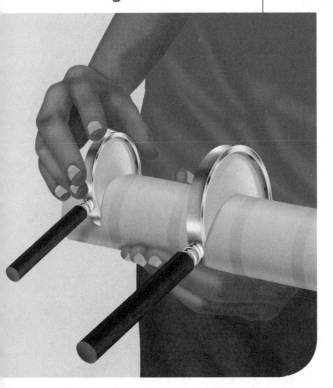

10 **Step 3:** Hold the two magnifying glasses steady, making sure to keep the newspaper in focus in the larger lens. Ask your friend to use the measuring tape to find the distance between the two magnifying glasses, and have him or her write down that number.

11 **Step 4:** Next, measure a distance of 1 inch (2.5 **centimeters**) from one end of the cardboard tube. Draw a line with the black marker, and use the scissors to cut a slot into the tube on the line you marked. Do not cut all the way through the tube. The slot should only be large enough to hold the big magnifying glass.

Figure B

12 **Step 5:** Now, measure the distance your friend wrote down from the slot on the tube. Draw a line with the marker, and cut another slot in the tube. This one should only be large enough to hold the small magnifying glass.

13 **Step 6:** Put the two magnifying glasses into their slots. Remember, the big one goes in the front and the small one goes in the back. Use the masking tape to hold the two lenses in place.

14 **Step 7:** Next, measure about 1 inch beyond the small magnifying glass. Draw a line with the marker. The rest is **excess** tube. Cut it off.

15 **Step 8:** Finally, test the telescope by looking at the piece of newspaper with it. You may need to adjust the distance between the two magnifying glasses to get the best quality.

Comprehension Check

1. What kind of image is Figure C?

    a. a chart

    b. a graph

    c. an illustration

    d. a photograph

2. What does Figure C show?

    a. It shows how to cut off the excess part of the tube.

    b. It shows how to put the magnifying lenses into place.

    c. It shows how to test the telescope to get the best quality.

    d. It shows how to measure 1 inch along the cardboard tube.

3. Work with a partner to discuss how Figure C connects to the text. What does the image show that the text does not say? How does Figure C help the reader?

    It shows what way the place is the direction.

Independent Practice

How to Make a Telescope *continued*

RI.3.7

WORDS TO KNOW

comet
constellation
crater

CITE EVIDENCE

A Underline the paragraph that explains what a constellation is and names the two best-known constellations.

B Which image on this page helps you understand the information in paragraph 19? Draw a box around the caption that explains what the image is.

16   Wait for a clear night to try out your telescope. Stare at the sky through the end with the two lenses. Any objects you see will appear upside down. That is how they looked to the astronomers who built the first telescopes.

17   Here are some things to observe with your new telescope.

18   **The Moon:** The moon is the largest object in the night sky. You can use your telescope to get a better look at **craters** on the moon's surface.

19   **Constellations:** A **constellation** is a collection of stars that forms a pattern. Two of the most well-known constellations are the Big Dipper and Orion.

20   **Planets:** There are seven other planets in the solar system. It is possible to see up to five of them in the sky at night: Mercury, Venus, Mars, Jupiter, and Saturn.

21   **Comets:** A **comet** is a huge ball of ice and dust, streaking across the sky. Comets are often named after the first person who reports seeing them, which is a good reason to look for them!

A comet

The Big Dipper

22   **Objects on Earth:** You can also use your telescope to view faraway objects right here on Earth. It is also great for bird watching or for studying landscapes in the distance. You might learn just as much about life on our planet as you do about outer space.

23   Keep a journal of the objects you see in your telescope. Record your observations, or draw illustrations of everything you see. It is another way to enjoy your homemade telescope!

Comprehension Check

MORE ONLINE   sadlierconnect.com

1. Circle the answer that completes the following sentence. The image of the Big Dipper shows you what _____ looks like.

(a.) a constellation

b. a comet

c. Orion

d. the moon's craters

2. Which text connects to what you see in the image of the comet?

a. Comets are named after the first person who finds them.

b. Keep a journal of the objects you see in your telescope.

c. There are seven other planets in the solar system.

(d.) A comet is a huge ball of ice and dust, streaking across the sky.

3. What does the image of the comet show that the text does not say? Why was the image included?

When the comet leaves you can see it's trail.

RI.3.8

WORDS TO KNOW

calculation
classification
gravitational pull
orbit

Text structure is the way a text is organized. Different texts can have different structures.

CITE EVIDENCE

A **Sequence** is one type of text structure. Sequence tells when things happened. In paragraph 1, underline an event that happened in 1930. Box an event that happened after.

B Sequence explains the **order of events in a series**. It tells which one happened first, which happened second, and so on. Circle the sentence that describes the discoveries of Uranus and Neptune. Which of these two planets was discovered first?

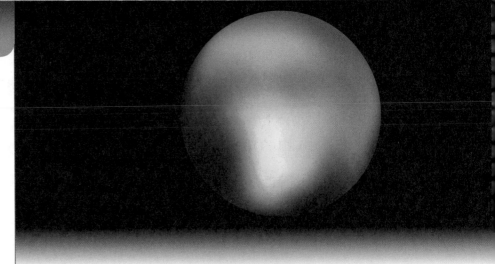

Pluto:
Planet or Not?
(Genre: Magazine Article)

1   The year was 1930. Astronomers in Arizona had discovered an unknown object in space. What was it? They were not sure. However, it seemed to behave like a planet, so it must be a planet. They declared it was the ninth planet in our solar system. It became known as Pluto.

2   For decades, that **classification** remained in place. But in 2006, everything changed. Scientists were no longer sure what to call Pluto. Was it a planet or not? Here is the strange story of the former planet Pluto.

The Search for "Planet X"

3   For years, students were taught the solar system contained nine planets: Mercury, Venus, Earth, Mars, Jupiter, Saturn, Uranus, Neptune, and Pluto. The last three planets were discovered across centuries as astronomers used increasingly sophisticated tools to study space. Uranus was discovered in 1781, and Neptune was found in 1846.

RI.3.8

4   About 50 years after Neptune's discovery, an astronomer named Percival Lowell suspected there might be a ninth planet in the solar system. So, in 1905, he decided to search for it. He called it "Planet X." Lowell spent more than a decade searching for this planet, but he could not find it.

The Discovery of Pluto

5   In 1929, an astronomer named Clyde Tombaugh was working at an observatory that Percival Lowell had founded in Arizona. He wondered if Percival Lowell might be right about a ninth planet in the solar system. So, he took up the search. He started with Lowell's **calculations** and then expanded his search.

6   The following year, Tombaugh's search uncovered a tiny, distant planet on the far edges of the solar system. It appeared no bigger than a bit of dust in a photograph. Could this be it? One clue was the **gravitational pull** of the unknown object, which affected the **orbits** of Neptune and Uranus.

CITE EVIDENCE

C **Cause and effect** is another type of text structure. A cause is the reason something happens, and the effect is what happened. Paragraph 4 uses this structure. Circle the effect of Lowell's suspicions in paragraph 4.

D Underline the sentence that tells what Tombaugh did when he first took up the search for Lowell's "Planet X." Why did Tombaugh expand his search?

Comprehension Check

Clyde Tombaugh decided to continue Percival Lowell's search. What was the effect? Include evidence from the text in your answer.

Percival Lowell

DESCRIBING TEXT STRUCTURES

Guided Practice

Pluto: Planet or Not? *continued*

RI.3.8

WORDS TO KNOW
gravity
universe

CITE EVIDENCE

A Clyde Tombaugh did not have to search as long as Percival Lowell did to find "Planet X." Underline the event that happened on March 13, 1930.

B Circle two things from paragraph 8 that occurred after March 13, 1930. In paragraph 9, circle the detail that tells you if the paragraph describes events from 1930 or refers to an earlier time.

7   **Gravity** is a force that acts to draw objects together. The bigger an object is, the greater the object's gravitational pull. Gravity on Earth pulls objects to the ground, which is a good thing. Without Earth's gravitational pull, everything on Earth would float into space! The impact of Pluto's gravitational pull on Neptune and Uranus was great enough to make scientists look for its source.

8   On March 13, 1930, the Lowell Observatory announced the discovery. This object was celebrated as the ninth planet in our part of the **universe**. An 11-year-old schoolgirl from England suggested the name *Pluto*, after the name of a Roman god. Her grandfather was friends with an astronomer and passed on her suggestion.

9   Unfortunately, Percival Lowell, who died in 1916, did not live to see the discovery of his mystery planet. But one reason the name *Pluto* was selected was because the first two letters are Percival Lowell's initials.

A Dwarf Planet

10   Pluto was called a planet for decades. Astronomers continued to study it. Around 1950, a scientist named Gerard Kuiper used a high-powered telescope to study Pluto. In 1978, other scientists discovered one of Pluto's moons. They named it Charon.

Mercury   Venus   Earth   Mars   Jupiter   Saturn   Uranus   Neptune   Pluto

11   Everything changed in 2006 when scientists decided to define the planets. Gravitational strength was a big part of this new definition, and Pluto no longer fit the definition of a planet.

Comprehension Check

1. What is the effect of Earth's gravity?

    a. It pushes against Pluto.

    (b.) It pulls objects to the ground.

    c. It makes objects float into space.

    d. It helps astronomers find new planets.

2. What information caused Pluto to be called a planet in the first place?

    a. Its gravitational pull was great enough.

    b. It was named after a Roman god.

    c. It had a moon called Charon.

    (d.) It was far out in space.

3. Work with a partner to discuss the events that occurred around 1950 and in 1978. What caused these events? Cite text evidence.

In 1950 Gerard Kuiper used a high-powerd telescope to study Pluto. In 1978 other scentists discoved one of plutos moons

DESCRIBING TEXT STRUCTURES

Independent Practice

Pluto: Planet or Not? *continued*

RI.3.8

WORDS TO KNOW

asteroid
dwarf planet
mnemonic

CITE EVIDENCE

A Underline the text that describes why some people think Pluto should still be called a planet.

B Draw a box around words in the first and last sentence in paragraph 16 that point to a sequence of events. Why was a new mnemonic needed?

12   In 2006, astronomers came up with new measurements for what makes something a planet. They said a planet had to have a certain level of gravity. Pluto did not meet that measurement. Its gravity was not strong enough to pull **asteroids** close or push them away.

13   Instead, Pluto became known as a **dwarf planet**, which is smaller than a regular planet. There are at least two other dwarf planets, Ceres and Eris. In fact, there might be many, many more.

14   Many people question the new classification. After all, Pluto does orbit the sun like the planets of the solar system. Yet size seems to matter the most, and Pluto is simply too small. Plus, it travels around the sun in a strange way. Also, sometimes Pluto passes in and out of Neptune's orbit. No other planets cross orbits with another planet.

Pluto Remains a Puzzle

15   Today, Pluto remains a puzzle for many people. Some think it should still be considered a planet. Others consider it to be only a dwarf planet. Still others believe it is somewhere in between. Will Pluto ever be a planet again? Its history shows that anything can happen. After all, 20 years ago, almost no one would have thought that the solar system would *lose* a planet.

RI.3.8

A Way to Remember

16   After 2006, we looked at Pluto in a new way. We also came up with a new **mnemonic** (nih-MAH-nik). A mnemonic is a phrase that helps you remember something. A mnemonic for the solar system used to be "My Very Educated Mother Just Served Us Nine Pies." The first letter of each word represents a planet. So "My" stood for Mercury, and so on. Now, many students use "My Very Educated Mother Just Served Us Noodles."

Comprehension Check

(MORE ONLINE) sadlierconnect.com

1. What happened in 2006 that changed Pluto to a dwarf planet?

    a. Scientists discovered Neptune.

    b. Scientists decided Ceres and Eris were dwarf planets.

    c. Scientists used new measurements to classify planets.

    d. Pluto failed to orbit the sun.

2. The author seems to suggest that because of its unpredictable past, Pluto could one day

    a. change in size.

    b. be named a planet again.

    c. change places with Neptune.

    d. drop out of the solar system.

3. Explain the decision astronomers made about Pluto in 2006. What was the cause of this decision? What was the effect?

    In, 2006 its gravity was not strong enough to pull asteroids close or push them away.

Guided Instruction

RI.3.9

WORDS TO KNOW
category
ellipse
interior

To **compare**, you look at how two or more things are alike. To **contrast**, you look at how they are different.

CITE EVIDENCE

A To **compare** or **contrast** two pieces on the same topic, it is necessary to find the **key details** in each. Box the paragraphs that give key details that describe Pluto.

B When comparing, see how details in the pieces are similar; when contrasting, see how they are different. Underline details about Pluto that did not appear in "Pluto: Planet or Not?" Do these details support the idea that Pluto is a planet?

Pluto Is Our Planet!
(Genre: Editorial)

1   We used to have nine planets: Mercury, Venus, Earth, Mars, Jupiter, Saturn, Uranus, Neptune, and Pluto. Pluto was discovered in 1930 and was a planet until 2006. Then scientists decided that Pluto was only a "dwarf" planet. It does not make sense to add this other **category** of planet. Pluto and the other dwarf planets are planets, too!

2   Pluto is very, very far away from the sun. It is in the Kuiper Belt, an area in space that is full of icy, rocky objects. Pluto is very small. It is only about two-thirds the size of Earth's moon. However, it has at least five moons. One, named Charon, is half as big as Pluto. The other moons are very small.

3   Pluto has a rocky core surrounded by ice. It takes 248 years for Pluto to go around the sun. It moves in an **ellipse**, so sometimes it is nearer to the sun than at other times. When it comes close to the sun, the ice on its surface melts and an atmosphere forms. When it moves farther away, the ice freezes again and the atmosphere disappears.

RI.3.9

4   Pluto is not the only dwarf planet. Another dwarf planet is named Eris. This little world is very similar to Pluto. It, too, has a rocky middle and icy outer surface. It is also about the same size. Eris is even farther from the sun than Pluto. Its orbit around the sun takes 557 years and moves Eris beyond the Kuiper Belt. It only has one known moon.

5   Ceres is yet another dwarf planet. It is in the asteroid belt between Mars and Jupiter. Ceres is only about the size of Texas, but it is more like a planet than an asteroid. It is rocky and nearly round, and it has a lot of water. Its **interior** is in layers like a planet. Astronomers at first called Ceres a planet, too. They then called it an asteroid before deciding it was a dwarf planet.

CITE EVIDENCE

C Look for clue words like *another*, *both*, and *too* that show comparison. Circle the comparison words in paragraph 4.

D Underline details that show how the dwarf planets Eris and Ceres are similar to Pluto. Were Eris and Ceres described in "Pluto: Planet or Not?"

Comprehension Check

Compare the details given here about Pluto to those given in "Pluto: Planet or Not?" Which are the same? Which are different? Cite text evidence.

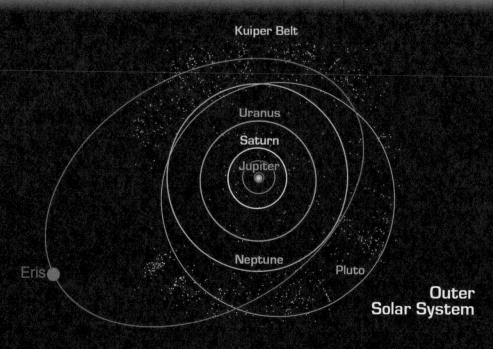

Kuiper Belt

Uranus

Saturn

Jupiter

Neptune

Pluto

Eris

Outer Solar System

COMPARING AND CONTRASTING TEXTS

Pluto Is Our Planet! *continued*

RI.3.9

WORDS TO KNOW

diameter

judging

CITE EVIDENCE

A Underline the clue words that show a contrast is being made in paragraph 8.

B Circle the name of the planet that is close in size to Pluto. Did the other article discuss the similar size of this planet and Pluto?

6   Pluto and the other dwarf planets *are* different in some ways. But the dwarf planets are not different enough to be in their own group. In fact, in many ways the dwarf planets are more similar to the interior planets, Mercury, Venus, Earth, and Mars, than these planets are to the outer planets of our solar system.

7   The name *dwarf planet* makes it seem as if these objects are simply too small to be planets. But this is not true. They are small, but the planet Mercury has a **diameter** similar to that of Earth's moon. Pluto is much more similar in size to Mercury than Mercury is to any of the outer planets. Mercury and Venus have no moons. Earth has one, and Mars has only two. These interior planets are small and have only a few moons, just like Pluto.

8   On the other hand, the outer planets, Jupiter, Saturn, Uranus, and Neptune, are all much bigger than Earth. Jupiter is more than ten times bigger, Saturn nine times, and Neptune and Uranus almost four times bigger. All have many moons. Neptune has the fewest with 13. Saturn has at least 53! **Judging** simply by size, it seems that Earth and the inner planets are much more similar to each other and the dwarf planets. Maybe the outer planets should be called "giant planets"!

9 Pluto and the other dwarf planets are not big enough to clear asteroids out of their orbits. Instead, they are surrounded by other objects. This is the main difference scientists use to call them "dwarf planets." This difference is not nearly as important as the similarities between Pluto and the planets.

Comprehension Check

MORE ONLINE sadlierconnect.com

1. What does "Pluto: Planet or Not?" say about dwarf planets that this article does not?

   a. There is only one, Pluto.

   b. There might be many, many more.

   c. There are only two, Eris and Ceres.

   d. There are some as big as Mercury.

2. Contrast this article so far to the first one, "Pluto: Planet or Not?" How are they different?

   a. The first is an opinion piece; this one is nonfiction.

   b. The first is fiction; this one is nonfiction.

   c. They are not different; both are opinion pieces.

   d. The first is nonfiction; this one is an opinion piece.

3. What key point is the author making in this section? Compare and contrast how this point is discussed here and in "Pluto: Planet or Not?"

   It talks about Pluto.

Independent Practice

Pluto Is Our Planet! *continued*

RI.3.9

WORDS TO KNOW

core

tilted

CITE EVIDENCE

A Circle the clue words that signal comparison and contrast on this page.

B Underline the details that describe the qualities of the outer versus the inner planets. Did the other article also cover these details?

10   Pluto is not that different from Earth in how it is formed. Earth and the inner planets Mercury and Mars are mostly made up of rock. Their surfaces are surrounded by an atmosphere, although Mercury has only a very thin one. Pluto also has an atmosphere some of the time. It and the other dwarf planets are rocky, too.

11   However, the outer giants are different. They are not made up mostly of rock. Jupiter has a small, rocky **core** deep inside the planet, but most of it is made of gases like hydrogen and helium. Saturn is very similar to Jupiter, which is made of hydrogen and helium. Spaceships could not land on these planets! Uranus and Neptune are ice giants. Both have thick atmospheres as well. Both are **tilted** strangely to the side and are very, very cold.

12   It is clear that planets have a lot of differences. It is also clear that Pluto is more similar to Earth and the inner planets than the outer planets are. Saying that Pluto is not a planet makes little sense when it is compared to Earth, and Earth to Jupiter or Saturn.

Pluto

Rock and ice

Earth

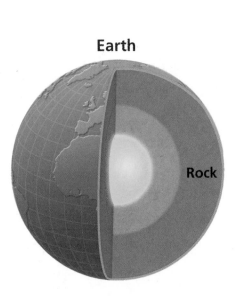

Rock

Saturn

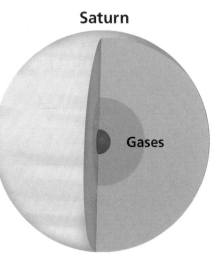

Gases

RI.3.9

13   Pluto deserves to be a planet. It is small, far away, and very cold, but it is still part of our solar system. Our solar system has room for planets as different as Mercury and Jupiter. It has room for Ceres, Eris, and especially for Pluto, too!

Comprehension Check

(MORE ONLINE) **sadlierconnect.com**

1. What does this article tell us about Uranus and Neptune that "Pluto: Planet or Not?" does not?

   a. They have rocky cores.

   b. They were discovered 65 years apart.

   c. They are ice giants.

   d. They are similar to Jupiter.

2. What does the author of "Pluto: Planet or Not?" tell us about Pluto that this opinion article does not?

   a. how Pluto was formed

   b. how Pluto first became a planet

   c. why Pluto was named a dwarf planet

   d. why Pluto should be a regular planet again

3. What key point is the author making in this section? Compare and contrast how this point is discussed here and in "Pluto: Planet or Not?"

   It is talking about the other plants

_____

_____

_____

HW

Why the Solar System Moves

(Genre: Explanatory Text)

1   Long ago, people thought the sun moved around Earth. The sun rose in the east and set in the west, so they thought it must be moving. They also saw that the sun was not the only object in the sky that moved. Most stars were still, but some moved. The ancient astronomers called these "wanderers," or "planets." They thought these planets moved around Earth, which was still, or unmoving.

2   In the early 1500s, however, the astronomer Nicolaus Copernicus began to suspect that Earth moved around the sun. It took a long time for this new idea to be accepted. The astronomer Galileo was even arrested for believing it! Slowly, however, more people began to understand this different idea of the universe.

3   Today, we know that Earth and the other seven planets move around the sun. Each moves in its own orbit. One trip, or revolution, around the sun can take anywhere from 88 days for Mercury to 165 years for Neptune. Also, everything in our solar system is spinning. The sun and all the planets rotate. There are different reasons for each of these movements, however. Everything has been spinning from the beginning of our galaxy, but the planets move around the sun because of gravity.

Hot, spinning gases and dust formed the sun.

RI.3.7, RI.3.8, RI.3.9, RI.3.10

4   Billions of years ago, our solar system was only a spinning cloud of dust and gas. Our galaxy is full of these clouds, which are called nebulas. Something made the nebula become thicker in the center. This change started a chain reaction. The dense center pulled more and more dust into it. Then, the cloud collapsed on itself and began to spin faster and faster. This momentum is like an ice skater moving more quickly as she pulls in her arms while spinning. The nebula flattened out into a spinning disc. The temperature became hotter and hotter. Finally, atoms of different gases reacted together in violent explosions. At this point, our sun was born.

5   The planets and other objects in our solar system were made when dust and gases swirled together. The same energy that spun the ancient cloud that became our solar system keeps everything in our solar system spinning to this day. The sun, planets, moons, and other objects in our solar system are always on the move.

6   These objects keep spinning because there is nothing in space to make them slow down or stop. Earth spins once per day. Mars spins at about the same rate. Mercury and Venus spin slowly. The giant, outer planets spin much more quickly. Even the sun spins. Some people think that Earth's moon does not rotate because the same side always faces Earth. In fact, the moon does spin, but it spins as it moves around our planet, so we only see one side of it.

All of the planets in our solar system orbit the sun.

7   Earth moves around the sun for a completely different reason than it rotates, or spins. The huge sun keeps the planets circling around it by gravity. Without the sun, Earth would use its spinning energy from its formation to zoom off into space. As Earth tries to move forward, the gravity of the sun pulls it in. As a result, Earth moves in a circle around the sun. The same thing happens with the other planets moving around the sun. Gravity is also the reason that moons orbit their planets!

8   Here is how one scientist described it: "Imagine that a very powerful robot was standing on top of a tall mountain holding a ball. The robot throws the ball. If you threw a ball, it would fall back to the ground. But this robot is so strong and throws the ball so far, it moves past the curve of Earth before it starts to fall. So there's nothing it can hit! It just keeps falling. However, it can't ever hit the ground because the ground curves away in front of it. At last the ball goes all around Earth, and the robot catches it again. This is how Earth moves around the sun. It is always falling in, but since there's nowhere to fall, it just keeps going."

9   Of course, a giant robot didn't throw Earth around the sun! But the original energy from our planet's creation acts as the "robot" that tossed Earth forward and keeps it moving around the sun.

10   Humans have come a long way. They once looked up at the sun and believed that it moved around Earth. Today, we have telescopes and powerful instruments. These instruments let astronomers look into the sky and work out details about how the universe works. These details also show how connected our world still is to the ancient past. Every new thing we learn brings our planet's beginnings a little closer.

11   The beginning of our solar system happened so long ago that it is hard to even imagine it. Yet the forces that created our system are still with us. The spin of our planet, which gives us day and night, is the same spin that created Earth in the first place. The planets move overhead, and our moon circles us because of those ancient forces. The movement of Earth around the sun that gives us the seasons of the year is directly tied to the creation of that same planet and star.

Comprehension Check

1. Reread paragraph 4. Which statement describes the first step in the birth of the sun?

   a. The cloud collapsed on itself.

   b. The nebula flattened out into a spinning disc.

   c. The nebula becomes thick at its center.

   d. Next, it started to spin faster and faster.

2. According to the text, what is the direct cause that created the sun?

   a. gravity from nebulas

   b. powerful robots spinning around

   c. Earth's motion left over from its creation

   d. atoms of different gases reacting and exploding

3. Use the information in paragraph 7 and the accompanying illustration to explain why Earth and other planets orbit the sun.

They orbit the sun because the huge sun
Keeps it spinning.

4. Compare and contrast the way information is presented in paragraphs 7 and 8. Which way better helped you understand why Earth orbits the sun? Why?

It is different because paragraph #7 is
talking about the planets spinning and it is
the same because it is talking about the
Earth in paragraphs 7 and 8.

RI.3.9, SL.3.1.a, SL.3.1.c, SL.3.1.d, SL.3.4

Compare and Contrast Texts

In this unit, you read about whether Pluto should be considered a planet and why the solar system moves. Think about what you learned from these texts and compare and contrast them using the T-chart below. List key details and important points from the texts to show the similarities and differences between them. Be prepared to discuss your ideas with your class.

Similarities	Differences

Return to the Essential Question

How can authors use text structure to connect ideas and information?

In small groups or as a class, discuss the Essential Question. Think about what you have learned about text illustrations, text structures, and comparing and contrasting texts. Use evidence from the four unit texts to answer the question.

L.3.5.c

Shades of Meaning

Guided Instruction Sometimes words have similar meanings, but they do not mean exactly the same thing. Instead, words have different shades of meaning—like different shades of blue in a box of crayons. Each word describes the same thing in a slightly different way. Compare the synonyms for the word *think* in the chart.

Guided Practice Refer to the chart. Answer *yes* or *no* to show whether or not there is evidence for each statement below.

_____ **1.** We <u>know</u> that Earth and the other planets move around the sun.

suspect	think based on clues or evidence
wonder	think about without evidence
believe	accept without evidence
know; understand	accept based on evidence

_____ **2.** Ancient people looked at the sun and <u>believed</u> it moved around Earth.

_____ **3.** Copernicus <u>suspected</u> that Earth moved around the sun.

Independent Practice Pick the correct synonym to complete each sentence below.

      suspect   **wonder**   **believe**

1. Children might _____ that the sun moves around Earth.

2. As scientists gathered evidence, they began to _____ that Pluto was not a planet.

3. Ancient people would _____ why stars seemed to move.

RI.3.7, RI.3.8, RI.3.9, L.3.5.c

Read the following passage, which includes illustrations and text features. Then answer the questions on pages 257 and 258.

Comets

(Genre: Scientific Text)

Comets

1   People once believed that comets were signs of something important about to happen. Today, we know that they are huge balls of frozen gases, like giant, dirty snowballs. As comets near the sun, they heat up. Because the comet gets warmer, some of the ice melts and a long tail blows out behind the comet. Astronomer Gerard Kuiper first suspected in 1951 that many comets come from a field of objects beyond Neptune. These comets orbit Earth at a great distance.

The Tale of a Tail

2   The tail of a comet is an amazing thing! It shines like a sword in the sky. No wonder ancient people thought it was an omen. At right, you can see how a comet's tail forms.

Fill in the circle of the correct answer choice.

1. What word in sentence 1 of paragraph 1 shows you that people had no evidence that comets were omens?

- ○ believed
- ◉ signs
- ○ about
- ○ know

2. Which word or phrase could best replace the word *know* in sentence 2 of paragraph 1?

- ○ suspect
- ○ believe
- ◉ have evidence to show us
- ○ do not have evidence to show us

3. What is the connection between sentences 3 and 4 in paragraph 1?

   ○ none

   ◉ cause and effect

   ○ steps in a sequence

   ○ comparison

4. Which other text in this unit has an image of a comet?

   ◉ "How to Make a Telescope"

   ○ "Pluto: Planet or Not?"

   ○ "Pluto Is Our Planet!"

   ○ "Why the Solar System Moves"

5. Underline the cause-and-effect clue word that connects sentences 3 and 4 in paragraph 1.

6. Circle the text and the image that describe the first step in the formation of a comet's tail.

7. What does a comet look like before it enters our solar system?

   A Giant dirty snow ball

8. According to the illustration, what causes the comet's tail to form?

   The long tail blows out

9. What are the most important points in "Comets" and "The Tale of a Tail"?

   Comets are formed

10. In your own words, explain the sequence of events described in the text and shown in the illustrations.

There are three parts to this performance task. Your teacher will provide you with copies of three selections.

- "The Summer of Sunflowers" Genre: Realistic Fiction
- "One Park for All to Enjoy" Genre: Nonfictional Narrative
- "Composting" Genre: Informational Text

Part 1: Literary Analysis

☐ Read "The Summer of Sunflowers" carefully. Take notes that will help you understand the passage.

☐ Answer Items 1–3 on pages 260–261.

☐ Then read the prompt for Item 4 and write a paragraph on your own paper. You may want to make some notes on scratch paper first.

Part 2: Narrative Writing

☐ Read "One Park for All to Enjoy" carefully. Take notes that will help you understand the passage.

☐ Answer Items 1–2 on page 262.

☐ Review "The Summer of Sunflowers." You will use both passages in this task.

☐ Then read the prompt for Item 3 and write an essay on your own paper. You may want to make some notes on scratch paper first.

Part 3: Research Simulation

☐ Read "Composting" carefully. Take notes that will help you understand the passage.

☐ Answer Items 1–3 on pages 263–264.

☐ Review "One Park for All to Enjoy." You will use both passages in this task.

☐ Then read the prompt for Item 4 and write an essay on your own paper. You may want to make some notes on scratch paper first.

LITERARY ANALYSIS

RL.3.1, RL.3.3, RL.3.4, RL.3.10, W.3.2, W.3.4, W.3.10, L.3.1, L.3.2, L.3.4.b

Part 1 Literary Analysis

Read all parts of the question before responding. Circle the correct answers to Items 1–3. Use your own paper to respond to Item 4.

Item 1

Part A   In "The Summer of Sunflowers," why was the narrator most upset?

a. Some sunflower seeds were taken by animals.

b. Some sunflower plants were added to the compost pile.

c. Some sunflower flowers were broken off the stem.

d. Some sunflower plants were taken by other gardeners.

Part B   Which sentence from the story supports the answer to Part A?

a. "Who is doing this?" I cried to Daddy.

b. "Sunflowers!" I shouted.

c. "At least the plants will do some good there," I said to myself.

d. When my plants started coming up, there were two or three crowded together in every spot!

Item 2

Part A   Read this exchange between the girl and her father.
"Do cats like sunflowers?" I asked.
"Yes," he answered shortly.
Which sentence is true about this brief conversation?

a. The father is angry with the daughter for asking so many questions.

b. The father is too upset at the situation to say very much.

c. The father is angry at the situation and thinking about how to fix it.

d. The daughter was just thinking aloud and didn't expect such a quick response.

Part B Which pair of words from the story are most helpful in understanding the conversation in Part A?

a. overjoyed, pretty

b. snapped, cried

c. carefully, glaring

d. stopped, flourished

Item 3

Part A What does the word **overabundance** mean in this sentence from "The Summer of Sunflowers"?

> They are the only ones in the garden, but I have an **overabundance**.

a. an incredibly strong support

b. an extremely large quantity

c. a very beautiful vision

d. a feeling of great joy

Part B Which sentence from the story best helps the reader understand the meaning of **overabundance**?

a. "In fact, I had so many sunflowers that I put a sign up on the community garden gate."

b. "So Daddy decided I should have the whole back row, along the fence."

c. "And like my sunflowers, I grew up this summer."

d. "The big, bright, yellow flowers were so pretty."

Item 4

How would you describe the girl's father in "The Summer of Sunflowers"? Decide three character traits that he has. Write a one-paragraph description of him that includes these traits. Use details from the story to explain why you think he has them.

Part 2 Narrative Writing

RL.3.6, RI.3.1, RI.3.4, RI.3.6, W.3.3, W.3.4, W.3.10, L.3.1, L.3.2, L.3.4.a, L.3.4.c

Read all parts of the question before responding. Circle the correct answers to Items 1–2. Use your own paper to respond to Item 3.

Item 1

Part A   Which sentence best describes the author?

a. The author is like a friend who appreciates your opinions.

b. The author thinks everyone should love Brook Run Park.

c. The author is a good "tour guide" for Brook Run Park.

d. The author knows what you enjoy about Brook Run Park.

Part B   Which sentence supports the answer to Part A?

a. "Our first stop is the Children's Adventure Garden."

b. ". . . Brook Run Park truly offers something for everyone."

c. "Children, teenagers, and adults were all involved . . ."

d. "To look at it now, you would never guess . . ."

Item 2

Part A   What does *residents* mean in this sentence from the text?
Park developers wanted . . . a place . . . for Dunwoody *residents*.

a. people who are very much alike

b. people who use things again and again

c. people who live in a certain place

d. people who design and build parks

Part B   Which phrase best helps readers understand *residents*?

a. "Park developers wanted to create"

b. "many people who reside in Dunwoody"

c. "Recycling is encouraged."

d. "you would like Brook Run to resemble"

Item 3

Write a new first paragraph for "The Summer of Sunflowers," in which you describe the setting as if it were Dunwoody Community Garden. Use details from the text. Describe the setting from the girl's point of view.

RI.3.1, RI.3.8, RI.3.9, RI.3.10, L.3.1, L.3.2, L.3.5.c, W.3.2, W.3.4, W.3.8, W.3.10

Part 3 Research Simulation

Read all parts of the question before responding. Circle the correct answers to Items 1–3. Use your own paper to respond to Item 4.

Item 1

Part A   What is the best way to describe how the information in "Composting" is organized?

a. sequence

b. comparison and contrast

c. opinion supported by fact

d. cause and effect

Part B   Which phrase from the text supports the answer to Part A?

a. "However, inside the compost pile"

b. "you would be correct"

c. "Because landfills are filling up so quickly"

d. "Your compost is now ready"

Item 2

Part A   Both "One Park for All to Enjoy" and "Composting" include guidance about how to compost. As you compare and contrast these directions, which statement is true?

a. "Composting" has information that anyone can use, but "One Park for All to Enjoy" includes some things that only Dunwoody gardeners would do.

b. Both sets of directions help readers understand how waste is turned into compost.

c. Only "Composting" points out how the process is good for the environment.

d. The same specific examples of green and brown wastes are given in both texts.

Part B   Which details from the texts support the answer to Part A?

a. Add brown waste on top. ("One Park for All to Enjoy")
   brown stuff such as leaves and pine needles ("Composting")

b. Place the scraps inside the cans found at the center of the
   wire cages. ("One Park for All to Enjoy")
   great compost is made of two basic things ("Composting")

c. the more good is done for the environment ("One Park
   for All to Enjoy") Composting is a great way to recycle
   ("Composting")

d. The directions are easy to follow. ("One Park for All to Enjoy")
   Worms are very helpful in composting piles. ("Composting")

Item 3

Part A   Read this sentence from "Composting."
   Have you ever *wondered* how you can change garbage into
   treasure?
   Think about how *wondered* fits in with words that describe
   degrees of certainty. Choose the group that *wondered* fits best.

a. wondered, believed, knew

b. wondered, felt, smelled

c. wondered, asked, said

d. wondered, read, wrote

Part B   Which words from the text support the answer to Part A?

a. You will know it is done

b. If you said "COMPOSTING,"

c. "Yuck!" you say?

d. when the dirt is crumbly and dark and smells earthy

Item 4

You have read two texts that give information about composting.
What two similar beliefs about composting do the authors of the
texts have? (Hint: Think about *how* to compost and *why*.) Write a
paragraph presenting these two beliefs. Include details from each
text that support these beliefs.

Foundational Skills Handbook

RF.3.3.a

Base Words

A **base word** is a complete word. It makes sense as a word on its own. Many words are formed by adding a prefix or suffix to a base word. Recognizing the base word in words that have these word parts can help you read the words.

*Our new puppy is so **playful**.*

The base word in *playful* is *play*. The suffix *-ful* has been added to *play* to form the word *playful*.

Look at the words in the More Words column. Notice that many words can be formed from the base word *play*.

Base Word	More Words
play	play**ing**
	play**er**
	replay

Read each sentence. Circle the base word in the underlined word. Then write two new words with the same base word. Add a different prefix or suffix to form each word.

1. We <u>preheat</u> the oven before we bake the bread.

   heating   heat

2. My math <u>teacher</u> lives down the street.

   teach   teaching

3. Our new neighbor was very <u>helpful</u> after the storm.

   helpful   helping

Choose one of the new words to write a sentence of your own.

4. I am helping my mom.

Prefixes

A **prefix** is a word part that is added to the beginning of a base word. A base word is a complete word. It makes sense as a word on its own. Adding a prefix creates a new word by adding to the meaning of a base word. One way to read unknown words is to look for a prefix.

> I **reread** my report to fix any mistakes.

The prefix in *reread* is *re-*. It comes at the beginning of the base word *read*. The prefix *re-* means "again." To reread a report means to read the report again.

Prefix	Meaning	Word	Meaning
re-	"again"	*re*pack	"pack again"
un-	"not" or "opposite of"	*un*kind	"not kind"
pre-	"before"	*pre*wash	"wash before"

Underline the prefix in each group of words. Then write the meaning of each word.

1. unlock   *not lock*

   unhappy   *not happy*

   untie   *not tie*

2. rebuild   *build again*

   refill   *to refill*

   repaint   *to pait again*

3. premix   *mix before*

   prepay   *pay before*

   preview   *veiw before*

In each sentence, underline the word with a prefix. Then take turns reading the sentences with a partner.

4. My aunt was <u>unable</u> to go to our school play.

5. I <u>recycle</u> bottles so they can be used again.

6. <u>Preheat</u> the oven before you bake the muffins.

7. Please <u>restate</u> your answer.

8. My little brother was <u>unaware</u> that I had borrowed one of his toys.

9. We took a <u>pretest</u> in school today so that we would know what to study.

RF.3.3.a

Suffixes

A **suffix** is a word part that is added to the end of a base word. A suffix creates a new word by adding to the meaning of a base word. One way to read unknown words is to look for a suffix.

*Someday I want to be a science **teacher**.*

The suffix in teacher is -er. It comes at the end of the base word *teach*. The suffix -er means "person who." A science teacher is a person who teaches science.

Suffix	Meaning	Word	Meaning
-ful	"full of"	play**ful**	"full of play"
-ly	"in a certain way"	safe**ly**	"in a safe way"
-er	"person who"	sing**er**	"a person who sings"

Underline the suffix in each group of words. Then write the meaning of each word.

1. farmer _Farm_

   builder _build_

   climber _climb_

2. cheerful _cheer_

   helpful _help_

   harmful _harm_

3. brightly _bright_

   quickly _quick_

   strongly _strong_

In each sentence, underline the word with a suffix. Then take turns reading the sentences with a partner.

4. Please be careful when you use scissors.

5. The painter used two colors to paint the kitchen.

6. We tiptoe into the room quietly.

7. The girl proudly crossed the finish line.

8. I was joyful because we were going to have a picnic.

9. The catcher caught the ball without even looking!

Latin Suffixes

The word parts -able, -ment, and -ion are also suffixes. Recognizing them in unknown words can help you read the words. These suffixes came from the Latin language.

Look at the words in the chart. Notice how separating the base word and Latin suffix makes it easier to read the words.

Word	Base Word	Suffix
agreeable	agree	-able
measurement	measure	-ment
correction	correct	-ion

Look at each group of words. Circle the suffix in each word. Then read the words.

1. statement   payment   improvement
2. direction   election   inspection
3. washable   breakable   bendable

In each sentence, underline the word with a suffix. Then take turns reading the sentences with a partner.

4. We spent an enjoyable day at the park.
5. The excitement of the day made me tired.
6. Look at our collection of rocks.
7. We watch the dolphins in amazement.
8. The computer is a great invention.
9. My quick movement may scare the cat.
10. Large print is more readable than small print.

RF.3.3.c, RF.3.4.c

Multisyllable Words: VCV

Sometimes a word has one consonant between two vowels. To figure out the word, divide it into syllables before the consonant and pronounce the first syllable with a long vowel sound. If you do not recognize the word, divide the word after the consonant and pronounce the first syllable with a short vowel sound.

open	habit	below	cabin
o-pen	h**ab-i**t	b**e-lo**w	c**ab-i**n

**Write each word, dividing it into syllables with a hyphen.
The first one has been done for you.**

1. over _____o-ver_____   6. river _____

2. idea _____   7. hero _____

3. clever _____   8. began _____

4. reward _____   9. beyond _____

5. visit _____ 10. decide _____

Choose the best word from the list above to complete each sentence. Then read this paragraph about a girl who rescues a cat.

As Gina _____ to take a bite of her fish sandwich, she heard cries outside. She looked out the window and saw that a cat was in her neighbor's tree _____ its owner's reach. Gina had an _____. She went _____ to her neighbor's yard. Hoping the cat would _____ to climb down to eat the sandwich, Gina put it on the ground. The cat came down! "Thank you for being such a _____ girl," the cat's owner said to Gina. "I will give you a _____." Gina shook her head and said, "Feeling like a _____ is enough for me!"

Multisyllable Words: VCCV

A **syllable** is a word part with one vowel sound. Multisyllable words are words with more than one syllable. When you see an unknown word, divide it into syllables. Doing this will help you figure out the word. If a word has two consonants between two vowels, you can usually divide it between the consonants.

signal	husband	blossom
sig-nal	**h**us-**ba**nd	bl**os-so**m

Write each word, dividing it into syllables with a hyphen. The first one has been done for you.

1. insect   _____in-sect_____
5. welcome   _____

2. coffee   _____
6. rescue   _____

3. sudden   _____
7. invite   _____

4. practice   _____
8. doctor   _____

Choose the best word from the list above to complete each sentence. Take turns reading the sentences with a partner.

9. Do you plan to _____ all of your cousins to your birthday party?

10. The ride's _____ starts and stops made it very thrilling.

11. All team members who miss _____ will not be allowed to play.

12. I am going to the _____ today for my yearly checkup.

13. Any _____ that crawled into the spider's web was trapped.

14. The other students gave Raquel a warm _____ on her first day.

15. My mother has a cup of _____ with her breakfast every morning.

16. The Coast Guard's bold _____ of the ship's passengers was on the news.

RF.3.3.c, RF.3.4.c

Multisyllable Words: -*le*

Sometimes a word ends in a consonant followed by -*le*. The -*le* and the consonant before it form a syllable. Recognizing this syllable can help you read words ending in a consonant followed by -*le*.

puzzle   table   candle
puz-**zle**   ta-**ble**   can-**dle**

Write each word, dividing it into syllables with a hyphen. The first one has been done for you.

1. sparkle   _spar-kle_   6. battle   _____
2. bubble   _____   7. simple   _____
3. purple   _____   8. dangle   _____
4. circle   _____   9. needle   _____
5. tumble   _____   10. gentle   _____

Choose the best word from the list above to complete each sentence. Take turns reading the sentences with a partner.

11. To make the color _____, mix red and blue.

12. "Jack and Jill" is a rhyme about children who _____ down a hill.

13. Tamika liked _____ clothes more than fancy dresses.

14. Before you can sew, you'll have to thread the _____.

15. The children chased the _____ so they could pop it.

16. My mother likes to _____ her feet in the pool, but I jump right in.

17. The glitter made the poster _____.

18. Please be _____ with the baby so he doesn't get hurt.

RF.3.3.d

Reading Irregularly Spelled Words

Words such as *said*, *enough*, and *beautiful* are words that you come across often when you read. These words have irregular spellings. They do not follow common spelling patterns. This makes the words hard to read.

Recognizing irregularly spelled words can help you read them quickly. Try looking for parts of words that have the same spelling. Sometimes these parts have the same pronunciation.

In each column, underline the part of each irregularly spelled word that has the same spelling. The first one has been done for you.

1. crumb	2. could	3. another	4. rough
numb	would	mother	tough
thumb	should	other	enough

Read the paragraph. Search for words from the list above. Write these words on the lines below.

When my brothers were little, they loved playing pranks. Every year on the day before April Fools' Day, they _____ come up with a prank. As if that wasn't bad _____, they would always try to get me to go along with them. Even though saying *no* was _____, I always did. Here are some of my favorites. Buy some cream-filled cookies and take the cream filling out. Then put toothpaste between the cookies instead. Be careful not to leave a single _____ in the bathroom, or your family will know that something is up! Here's _____ one. One year my brothers made a cake out of sponges. They covered the sponges with frosting and sprinkles. Then they told our _____ it was a special cake. She tried, but she _____ not cut it. I have to admit, our family had a lot of fun on April Fools' Day.

RF.3.4.a–c

Practicing Fluency

Read the following retelling of an Aesop fable. Use the checklist below to help guide your reading.

The Fox and the Goat

One day Fox stumbled into a well and couldn't escape. Eventually along came Goat, thirsty and sweaty. As he longingly peered into the well, Fox sweetly surprised him. "Welcome, Goat!"

"Greetings, Fox! Is the water fresh?" called Goat.

"It's the purest you'll ever taste," replied Fox cheerfully. "There's plenty to share, so come join me!"

Without thinking, Goat plunged into the well and drank his fill.

"Now that we are refreshed, let's leave," Fox said.

Goat looked up, crying, "Oh, no! How will we climb out?"

"With my clever plan!" answered Fox. "Press your feet against the stones that line the well. I'll climb your back, hop out, and fetch help."

Goat agreed gladly. Fox scampered up Goat's back, bounced off his horns, and was free. Before disappearing, he scolded Goat. "Foolish animal! Don't you know to look before you leap?"

Now read the story aloud to a partner. Use the checklist below and your understanding of the story to guide your reading.

Reading Checklist

- [ ] Does my voice go up if there is a question mark? Does it get stronger if there is an exclamation point? Do I pause for periods and commas?

- [ ] How should a character's thoughts or words affect how I read?

- [ ] How does the tone or mood of the story—suspenseful, scary, sad, happy—change the way I read? (Remember, the tone or mood can change more than once in a story.)

Writing Handbook

WRITING HANDBOOK

W.3.2, W.3.4,
W.3.5, W.3.6,
W.3.7, W.3.8

This year, you will write fiction and nonfiction narratives. You will also write an informative/explanatory text, an opinion piece, and a research report. This handbook is your guide to writing. It takes you through the steps of the writing process. These steps help you move from ideas to a finished piece of writing. Once you know the steps, you can use them for any kind of writing.

STEP 1 Planning

Let's say you are going to write an informative/explanatory essay for school about the four different types of clouds. Good writing begins with planning. To plan, begin by asking yourself some questions.

- **What** am I writing?

  In this assignment, you are writing a type of essay that provides information or explains something. It is nonfiction because it is about actual, or real, people, places, events, or ideas.

- **Why** am I writing? What is my **purpose**?

  Your purpose for writing is your reason for writing.
  For this assignment, your purpose is to inform. You will do this by explaining the four different kinds of clouds.

- **Who** is my audience? Who will read my writing?

  In this case, your audience is anybody who wants to learn about clouds.

> **RESEARCH TIP**
>
> When you research a topic, you gather information about it. You can use sources such as magazines, books, and online resources. You can even interview an expert. Be sure to take notes from the sources you use. Sort the information in the notes to help you organize your writing.

Then, think of ideas and organize them. An outline is one way to plan.

- Begin with your **big idea**.

  For informational text, begin with your **topic**—the central idea of your writing. Ask yourself, "What facts do I know about my topic that I can use?"

  For fiction, you might begin with the problem in the story that requires a solution.

- Then add **details**.

  For informational text, add ideas and facts that support your topic. Often, finding the ideas and facts requires research.

Here's what an outline for your essay on clouds might look like.

For fiction, add characters, setting, and plot events to your outline.

> Types of Clouds
>
> I. Introduction
>   Topic: Clouds come in many shapes and sizes, but scientists have identified four basic types.
>
> II. Explanation
>   Topic 1: Cumulus Clouds
>   Facts:
>   _____
>   _____
>
>   Topic 2: Stratus Clouds
>   Facts:
>   _____
>   _____
>
>   Topic 3: Cirrus Clouds
>   Facts:
>   _____
>   _____
>
>   Topic 4: Nimbus Clouds
>   Facts:
>   _____
>   _____
>
> III. Conclusion
>   _____
>   _____

PLANNING TOGETHER

- A partner can help you to get your ideas flowing.
- You might brainstorm together. Let one idea lead to the next.

WRITING HANDBOOK

W.3.4, W.3.5, W.3.6, W.3.10

STEP 2 Drafting

When you draft, you do the actual writing of your essay. Many writers use a computer to write drafts. Follow your outline, but don't worry about making everything perfect. Just write and get your ideas down!

Here is a handwritten draft of an essay about the different kinds of clouds. This is a great start!

Types of Clouds

Clouds come in many, many shapes and sizes. However, scientists have identified four basic types. The types have Latin names: cumulus, stratus, cirrus, nimbus.

Cumulus means "heap." You usually see these puffy white clouds when the weather is fair. However, they can change quickly when hot air pushes them up. Then a thunderstorm might happen.

Stratus means "layer." These gray clouds are flat. They go across the sky. Light rain might fall from them.

Cirrus means "curl of hair." These thin, wispy clouds are high in the sky. They made of ice. You can watch them move, like streamers.

Nimbus means "rain." If these dark clouds are up overhead, you are probably experiencing rain or snow.

Now you know more about clouds. They are more than shapes in the sky.

W.3.4, W.3.5, W.3.6, L.3.1.i, L.3.3.a

STEP 3 Revising

During this step, you think about how to make your writing better. This step is about ideas, not about spelling and grammar. Focus on the items in the checklist below. Your goal is to check each item. Then make changes on your computer or on a handwritten copy. If you are using pencil and paper, make a fresh copy.

REVISING TOGETHER

- You can work with a partner during revising. Have your partner read your draft and use a checklist to give you feedback. Use your partner's feedback to improve your draft.

- Finally, read your revised draft aloud to yourself or to your partner. See if you want to make any more improvements.

REVISING CHECKLIST

Ideas and Voice
- ☐ Do all of my ideas support my topic?
- ☐ Have I developed my ideas by including enough details?
- ☐ Does my writer's voice sound interesting and believable?

Organization and Coherence
- ☐ Does each idea fit with those before and after it?
- ☐ Have I used clue words to help readers follow the sequence or order of my ideas?
- ☐ Have I used a variety of sentence types?

Word Choice
- ☐ Have I avoided using the same words over and over?
- ☐ Do my words bring my ideas to life?

W.3.4, W.3.5, W.3.6, L.3.1.i, L.3.3.a

Here is a draft with notes for revisions. To see the revised draft, turn to page 282.

> In my next draft, I want to draw in the reader with a stronger introduction.

Types of Clouds

Who hasn't stared at the sky and found clouds that look like ~~When we look at the sky, it seems like there are a million~~ people or animals? Clouds do come in many, many shapes and sizes. ~~different types of beautiful clouds.~~ However, scientists have identified four basic types. The types have Latin names: <u>cumulus</u>, <u>stratus</u>, <u>cirrus</u>, <u>nimbus</u>.

<u>Cumulus</u> means "heap." You usually see these puffy white clouds when the weather is fair, ~~However,~~ but they can change quickly when hot air pushes them up. Then a thunderstorm might happen.

> I'm going to combine two sentences here to make my writing flow more smoothly.

<u>Stratus</u> means "layer." These gray clouds are flat, and they move across the sky. Light rain might fall from them.

<u>Cirrus</u> means "curl of hair." These thin, wispy clouds are high in the sky. They made of ice. You can watch them move, like streamers.

<u>Nimbus</u> means "rain." If these dark clouds are up overhead, you are probably experiencing rain or snow. So now when you study the clouds, you can call them by their ~~Now you know there are four basic types of clouds.~~ Latin names. You can also make smart guesses about the ~~Each one is different. They are more than just shapes in~~ weather. Of course, you can still have fun finding faces or ~~the sky.~~ shapes in the clouds you see.

> My conclusion needs to have more information about the topic.

STEP 4 Editing

This step is about making your writing correct. Now is the time to focus on grammar, punctuation, and spelling. Read your revised draft carefully. Sometimes it helps to read it aloud. Use the checklist to correct your writing on the computer or your handwritten draft.

EDITING CHECKLIST

Sentences

☐ Every sentence is a complete sentence. I have corrected any sentence fragments or run-on sentences.

Grammar

☐ The subject and verb of every sentence agree.

☐ The verb tense stays the same throughout.

☐ Pronouns match the nouns they replace.

Mechanics

☐ Every sentence begins with a capital letter and ends with the correct punctuation mark.

☐ Commas, quotation marks, and other punctuation marks are used correctly, and no marks are missing.

☐ The title and all proper nouns are capitalized.

☐ Paragraphs are indented.

Spelling

☐ I have used a dictionary to check spellings I am unsure about.

☐ I have correctly used any homophones (words that sound the same, such as *their/there/they're*).

W.3.5, W.3.6, L.3.1.f, L.3.2.a, L.3.2.g

PROOFREADING MARKS

Always proofread and correct your own work. Seeing your own mistakes can be difficult, though. Asking a partner to check your work can help.

∧	Add	ℒ	Take out	/	Small letter
⊙	Period	≡	Capital letter	○	Spelling error

Types of Clouds

Who hasn't stared at the sky and found clouds that look like people or animals? Clouds do come in many, many shapes and sizes. However, scientists have identified four basic types. The types have Latin names: <u>cumulus</u>, <u>stratus</u>, <u>cirrus</u>, <u>nimbus</u>.

<u>Cumulus</u> means "heap." you usually see these puffy white clouds when the weather is fair, but they can change quickly when hot air pushes them up. Then a thunderstorm might happen.

<u>Stratus</u> means "layer." These gray clouds are flat, and they seam to stretch across the sky. Light rain might fall from ȿtratus clouds.

<u>Cirrus</u> means "curl of hair." These thin, wispy clouds are high in the sky. They are made of ice. You can watch them move, like streamers⊙

<u>Nimbus</u> means "rain." If these dark clouds are up overhead, you are probably experiencing rain or snow.

So now when you study the clouds, you can call them by their Latin names. You can also make smart guesses about the weather. Of course, you can still have fun finding faces or shapes in the clouds you see.

W.3.6, SL.3.4, SL.3.6, L.3.3.a, L.3.3.b, L.3.6

STEP 5 Producing, Publishing, and Presenting

Now that you've worked so hard on your writing, it's time to share it with others! Think about how your writing looks. Is it neatly handwritten or typed and printed from the computer?

Would images add interest?
- photographs
- illustrations

Would text features make your ideas easier to understand?
- diagrams
- graphs
- charts
- maps

Think about the final form of your writing. Be sure the way you present your final version fits your purpose and audience.

DIGITAL CONNECTION

Technology makes it easy to present your writing to a bigger audience, especially on the Internet.

You might be asked to share your writing orally with others. Follow these rules to make your oral presentation effective.

- If you are changing a written essay into an oral presentation, make changes in words and in sentences that will help you talk to your audience. The language used for writing and speaking is not always the same.
- Use visuals as needed to support what you say.
- Speak clearly and loudly enough for everyone to hear.
- Speak slowly enough so that everyone can understand you.
- Make your gestures and facial expressions match your words.
- Change your voice at times, just as when you speak in real life.
- Be prepared to answer questions after your presentation.

LISTENING TIP

- Keep your eyes on the presenter, and focus your mind on the ideas.
- Make connections from what you hear to what you already know.
- Take notes. Include questions you want to ask.
- Try to picture the things that are described.

GLOSSARY

A

abnormal strange; weird

absorb to take in something; suck up

adapted changed to fit a new situation

admiring looking at something with enjoyment

anew again

applaud clap

approaching coming closer

assign give; appoint

asteroid space object made of rock

astronomer a person who studies the stars and planets

atmosphere the layer of air that surrounds Earth

B

bait food used to catch an animal

barrier wall or other structure that blocks off something

biology way an animal's body works

bloodshot red

bond connection; attachment

bragging boasting; being conceited

C

cactus a plant with thick stems and sharp thorns

calculation the use of math or logic to figure something out

category group, class

cave-in collapse of a mine tunnel

Centaur a mythical creature that is half human, half horse

centimeter a small unit of measurement

chamber room

civilization society; culture

classification the placing of similar objects in groups; organization

cloning using science to make a copy of a living thing

comet an icy object in space that sometimes forms a tail

commotion loud noise

condense shrink; come together

condition the state something or someone is in; situation

conserving saving; using less of something

constellation a group of stars that seems to make a picture

constructed built

contaminated dirty or unhealthy

continent giant landmass such as North America, Asia, or Australia

core center

crater hole; hollow

crew team; staff

culture a group's way of life and beliefs

D

dangerous something that can be harmful

debris broken pieces; trash

demonstration example; showing

despair hopelessness; sadness

destroy knock down; wreck

devastating causing terrible harm

diameter the distance across a circle or sphere

digestive system system in the body that processes food

disaster terrible event

DNA genes

dominated ruled over; controlled

dwarf planet a space object smaller than a planet and bigger than an asteroid

E

ellipse an oval shape

embarrassed made self-conscious

endangered rare; in danger of vanishing

enormous huge

environment nature; surrounding area

evaluate examine and make a decision

evidence proof; facts

excavate dig up

excess extra

exhibit display; show

expedition a group of explorers

expert skilled and knowledgeable

exploration discovery

expression look on someone's face

extinct when a species of plant or animal is no longer alive

F

focused paying attention to; concentrated

G

gravitational pull the pull of an object's gravity on another object

gravity the pull each object has on another object; larger objects have stronger gravity

grief great sadness; heartache

H

hammock a sling bed, often made of net

hatchling baby bird

healthy well and strong

hinge attachment that allows something, such as a door, to bend or open

GLOSSARY

I

imperiously bossily, commandingly

instructor teacher

interfere get in the way

interior inner, inside

intervened stepped in to take action

invention coming up with new ideas

investigate look into something

invisible when something can't be seen

irrigation watering

isolated alone

J

judging making a decision

L

labor work

lay claim assert a right to or ownership of something

levee a ridge or wall along a river to stop flooding

log book notebook that contains a list or record of activities

M

mammoth extinct hairy elephant

massive huge

mature grown-up; adult

mnemonic a clue to help you remember something

mobility ability to move around

mummy a dried body wrapped in bandages

murmur whisper; hum of voices

N

nonprofit organization a business with the goal of helping people, not making money

O

observation noticing things

offering gift given to a god to ask for his or her blessing

onlooker person watching

orbit path around the sun

orientation knowing where you are and how to go

original beginning, first

outdrilled drilled better than

outrage great anger

outskirts edges, borders, limits

P

prairie grassy plains

precious valuable, often also hard to find

precise careful, detailed

predict guess what will happen next

prehistoric happening before written history; ancient

preserved kept carefully; protected

proportion true importance or size; to blow something out of proportion is to make it a bigger deal than it is

prospect possibility; idea

proteins important, tiny parts of plants and animals

R

react respond; act

reflecting telescope an instrument that uses mirrors to look at faraway objects

refracting telescope an instrument that uses lenses to look at faraway objects

review look over again

royal belonging to a king or queen

ruins old, fallen-down buildings and towns

S

sandbar a ridge of sand in a river or lake

sarcophagus a kind of coffin

separated taken away from each other

severe strong; terrible

skeleton bone structure inside an animal's body

snowmelt water from melting snow

solar system the system of the sun and the planets and other orbiting objects

specialist an expert in a certain field

spirit attitude; quality; essence

spotlight attention; time on stage

stealthy quiet and sneaky

steam-powered run by steam instead of electricity or human power

strum to run a hand over strings on a musical instrument

sulked pouted; got in a bad mood

suspense anxious waiting

swooped flew suddenly; pounced

system arrangement, organization

T

theory idea about how or why something happened

tilted slightly turned

tombs graves; places where people are buried

tradition custom; something that has been done the same way for generations

treasure value greatly; find very important

U

ultimate greatest; best possible

universe everything that exists in space

university college

V

vapor mist; haze

vein line of mineral through rock

W

wildfire fire that burns wild land

wildlife wild animals

INDEX